HOW TO BUILD
WORKBENCHES
SAWHORSE TOOL CHEST
other build-it-yourself projects

by Donald R. Brann

Library of Congress Card No. 66-30452

SIXTH PRINTING – 1974

REVISED EDITION

Published by
DIRECTIONS SIMPLIFIED, INC.

Division of
EASI-BILD PATTERN CO., INC.
Briarcliff Manor, N.Y. 10510

All metric dimensions shown are approximate. Note page 65.

NOTE

Due to the variance in quality and availability of many materials and products, always follow directions a manufacturer and/or retailer offers. Unless products are used exactly as the manufacturer specifies, its warranty can be voided. While the author mentions certain products by trade name, no endorsement or end use guarantee is implied. In every case the author suggests end uses as specified by the manufacturer prior to publication.

Since manufacturers frequently change ingredients or formula and/or introduce new and improved products, or fail to distribute in certain areas, trade names are mentioned to help the reader zero in on products of comparable quality and end use.

The Publisher.

There's Magic
in Movement

Did you ever watch a bee buzz a flower, then light, search, and find food; a gull hover, then plunge and come up with a mouthful of fish? Everything the eye can see, and much more too small to discern, is in continual movement. Nothing remains motionless except that which we want to believe is so.

The mind, like all particles of microscopic matter, constantly shifts, forms new views, sees the same thing from many different angles. Changes constantly come, hover around us, plunge or pass through every gyration of thought, sight and feeling the mind can absorb. We instinctively try to adjust to every situation, regardless of whether it's material, mental, physical or theoretical.

The moments, minutes, hours, days and weeks we spend worrying about situations that may or may not happen, or have already happened, consumes a substantial part of our total inheritance of time.

The next time you find yourself enmeshed in a problem you can't solve, don't try stopping a change over which you don't exercise full control. Accept, side-step, or forget it for a time. Allow change to happen. It always does. Focus your mind, physical and mental energy on something else. Keep busy, keep doing something that requires attention. Allow time, and the magic of movement to carry you through.

Don Brann

This Book Simplifies Building

||||||||||||||||||||||||||||||||||||||||||||||||||||||||||||||||

6 FT. WORKBENCH

||||||||||||||||||||||||||||||||||||||||||||||||||||||||||||||||

CHILD'S SIZE BENCH

||||||||||||||||||||||||||||||||||||||||||||||||||||||||||||||||

FOLDAWAY BENCH

||||||||||||||||||||||||||||||||||||||||||||||||||||||||||||||||

TABLE TOP WORKBENCH

||||||||||||||||||||||||||||||||||||||||||||||||||||||||||||||||

SAWHORSE TOOL CHEST

||||||||||||||||||||||||||||||||||||||||||||||||||||||||||||||||

OTHER BUILD–IT–YOURSELF PROJECTS

||||||||||||||||||||||||||||||||||||||||||||||||||||||||||||||||

SIX FOOT WORKBENCH

This book simplifies building a well-planned 6 ft. workbench, a child's size, as well as a foldaway bench. Construction of a table top workbench is also explained. Each can be built from stock size lumber. Step-by-step directions explain and illustrate every step.

The three benches provide an economical solution to many problems. Because of their popularity, anyone interested in a spare time business will find these benches easy to sell. When offered for sale at fund raising church bazaars it's a popular seller. The tabletop bench has special appeal.

7

A child's size, equally rugged in construction, can also be built following directions provided. If you feel the bench is too high for a young child, build a platform using 2x4 on edge and ¾" plywood. This will raise child about 4", thus allow him to grow 4" before he fits bench.

The third bench, a foldaway design, is ideal for small space, in apartments, a boy's room, den, even a closet. Its design appeals to craftsmen in every line of activity from jewelry making, woodworking, ceramics to gardening and sewing. As directions suggest, this bench can be converted into a model railroad platform, a layout table for fabrics and patterns, to potting plants.

Building your own workbench, not only provides an economical solution to a problem, but also offers hours of escape and more hours of complete relaxation every time you use it.

Select the one you want to build, then read step-by-step directions through completely before cutting any lumber. Due to the variance in lumber width and thickness, after you assemble Legs A and B to Rails CDE and F, Illus. 2, check length required for other framing members. This permits cutting parts more accurately.

For great strength and rigidity, apply glue to all permanent wood-to-wood joints. Dip screws in glue before driving. Wipe excess glue away with a damp rag before it's allowed to set up.

Select straight lengths of kiln dried lumber, surfaced four sides (S4S). If lumber has small tight knots, paint knots with glue. For the purpose of this project, we figured surfaced lumber as measuring — 2x6 — 1½x5½"; 2x4 — 1½x3½"; 1x6 — ¾x5½"; 1x8 — ¾x7¼", 5/4" lumber will run from 1⅛" to 1¹/₁₆" thick. 1x1 is figured as measuring ¾x¾".

LIST OF MATERIALS

3 pcs. 2 x 6 x 12 ft. for A, B, G
1 pc. 2 x 6 x 10 ft. for A, C, E
1 pc. 2 x 6 x 5 ft, for C, B
1 pc. 2 x 4 x 10 ft. for D, F
1 pc. 1 x 6 x 12 ft. for L, K
1 pc. 1 x 6 x 10 ft. for K, J
1 pc. 1 x 8 x 4 ft. for M, N, O, P
1 pc. ¾ x 24 x 51″ Plywood for H
1 pc. ¼ x 24 x 40″ Plywood for Q
Sixty 1″ No. 8 Flathead Wood Screws
Twenty-four 1½″ No. 10 Flathead Wood Screws
Sixteen 2″ No. 10 Flathead Wood Screws
Nine 2½″ No. 10 Flathead Wood Screws
Twenty 2¾″ No. 12 Flathead Wood Screws
Sixteen 3″ No. 14 Flathead Wood Screws
Six ⅜ x 4″ Carriage Bolts, Washers, Nuts†

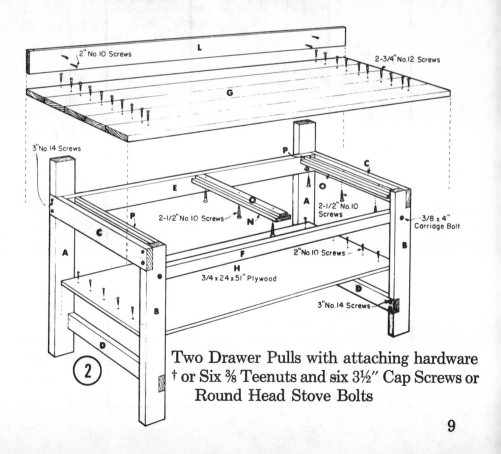

2″ No. 10 Screws
2-3/4″ No.12 Screws
L
G
3″ No. 14 Screws
P
C
E
O
A
2-1/2″ No. 10 Screws
N
2-1/2″ No.10 Screws
3/8 x 4″ Carriage Bolt
C
B
A
F
2″ No.10 Screws
H
3/4 x 24 x 51″ Plywood
B
D
3″ No.14 Screws
D

② Two Drawer Pulls with attaching hardware
† or Six ⅜ Teenuts and six 3½″ Cap Screws or
Round Head Stove Bolts

Cut two 2x6x39″ for back legs A, Illus. 2, 3. Cut 1½x5½″ notch, 6⅝″ from top end. Cut 1½x3½″ notch, 5″ from bottom.

3-1/2"	8.9 cm
5"	12.7
5-1/2"	14.0
6-5/8"	16.8
32-3/8"	82.2
39"	99.1

ALWAYS CUT NOTCHES TO FIT LUMBER YOU PURCHASE.

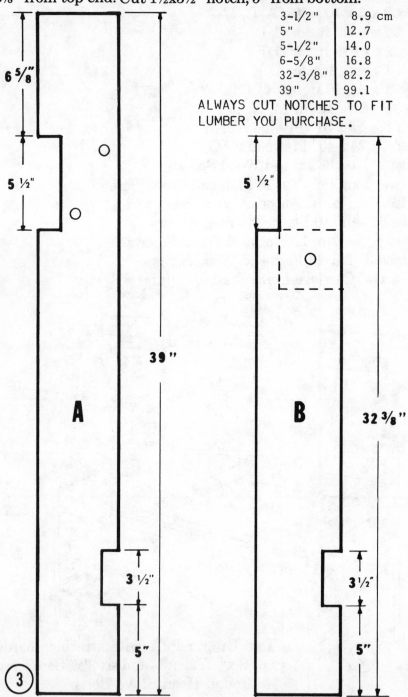

6⅝″

5 ½"

39″

A

B

32⅜″

5 ½"

3 ½"

3 ½"

5″

5″

③

10

Drill two ⅜″ holes (e), in position indicated, Illus. 4.

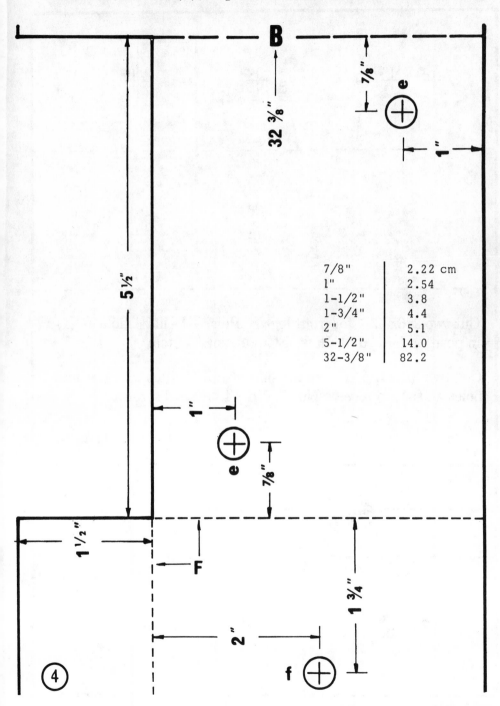

7/8"	2.22 cm
1"	2.54
1-1/2"	3.8
1-3/4"	4.4
2"	5.1
5-1/2"	14.0
32-3/8"	82.2

11

NOTE: If 2x6 you purchase measures 1⅝x5⅝" cut notches to fit.

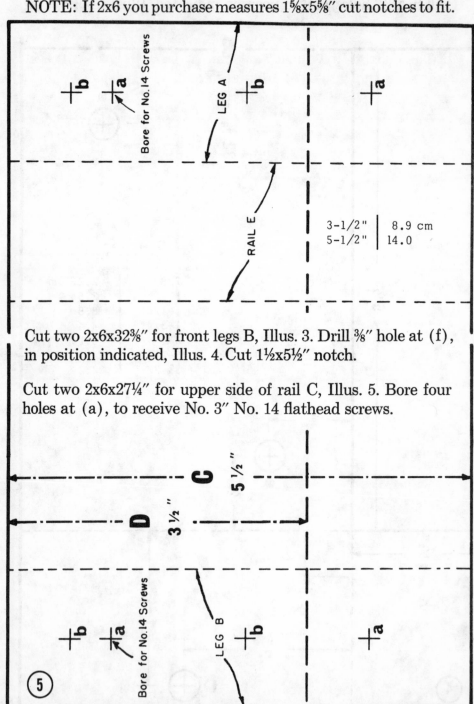

Bore for No.14 Screws

LEG A

RAIL E

| 3-1/2" | 8.9 cm |
| 5-1/2" | 14.0 |

Cut two 2x6x32⅜" for front legs B, Illus. 3. Drill ⅜" hole at (f), in position indicated, Illus. 4. Cut 1½x5½" notch.

Cut two 2x6x27¼" for upper side of rail C, Illus. 5. Bore four holes at (a), to receive No. 3" No. 14 flathead screws.

C

5 ½"

D

3 ½"

Bore for No.14 Screws

LEG B

⑤

Cut two 2x4x27¼″ for lower side rail D, Illus. 5. Bore four holes for No. 14 screws where indicated at (b).

Cut one 2x6x51″ for upper back rail E, Illus. 6. Drill two ⅜″ holes where indicated (e) from each end.

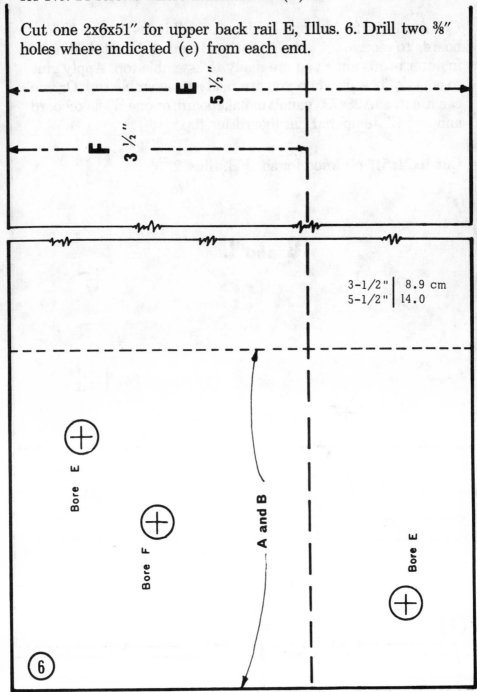

3-1/2″	8.9 cm
5-1/2″	14.0

Cut one 2x4x51" for upper front rail F, Illus. 6. Bore one ⅜" hole, where indicated from each end.

Cut five 2x6x72" for top G, Illus. 7. Drill holes at (g) in four boards to receive 2¾" No. 12 flathead screws. Don't drill holes in outer board until you are ready to assemble top. Apply glue to edges of boards when you are ready to assemble top. Or you can use two ¾x28x72" panels of flakeboard, or one ¾" flakeboard and one ¼" tempered hardboard for top.

Cut ¾x24x51" plywood for shelf H, Illus. 2.

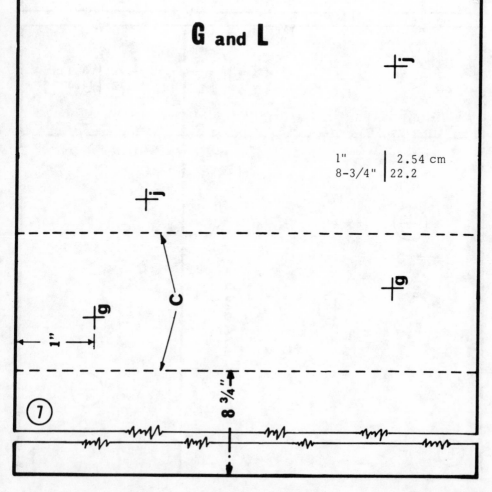

G and **L**

1"	2.54 cm
8-3/4"	22.2

⑦

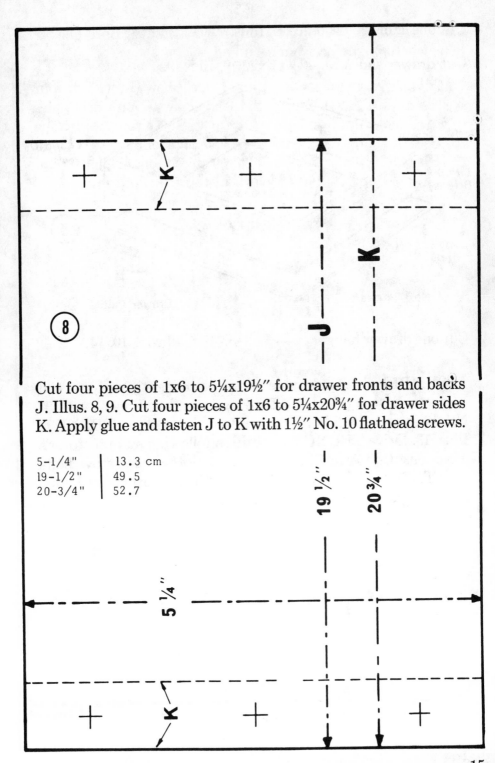

Cut four pieces of 1x6 to 5¼x19½″ for drawer fronts and backs J. Illus. 8, 9. Cut four pieces of 1x6 to 5¼x20¾″ for drawer sides K. Apply glue and fasten J to K with 1½″ No. 10 flathead screws.

5-1/4"	13.3 cm
19-1/2"	49.5
20-3/4"	52.7

Cut one 1x6x72″ for fence L, Illus. 7.

Cut drawer slides M — ½x¾x22¼″, Illus. 9.

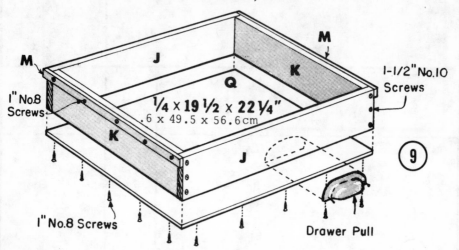

Cut one drawer hanger N — ¾x2⅝x22¼″, Illus. 2, 10, 14.

ASSEMBLY — Apply glue to all permanent wood-to-wood contacts. Fasten rail C and D to legs A and B, Illus. 2, with 3″ No. 14 screws. Drill holes to countersink shank on TEENUT, Illus. 13. Drive TEENUT in position following manufacturer's directions. Bolt A to E with four ⅜x4″ slotted head stove bolts with TEENUTS, or use ⅜x4″ carriage bolts, washers and nuts. Fasten shelf H to D with 2″ No. 10 screws.

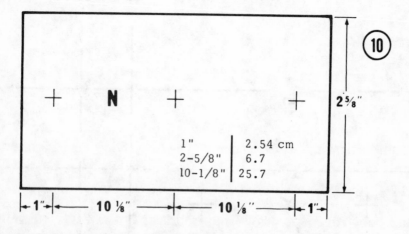

Cut three drawer hanger strips O — ¾x1⅝x22¼″, Illus. 2, 11, 14.

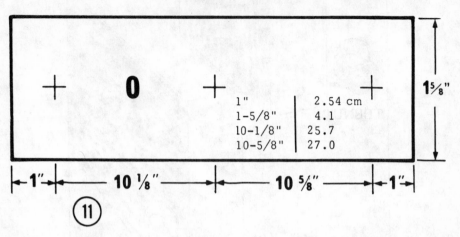

1″	2.54 cm
1-5/8″	4.1
10-1/8″	25.7
10-5/8″	27.0

Cut two drawer hanger strips P — ¾x1¼x22¼″, Illus. 12.

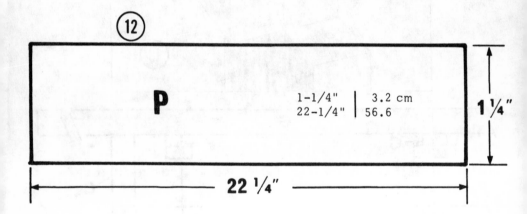

1-1/4″	3.2 cm
22-1/4″	56.6

Cut two drawer bottoms Q — ¼x19½x22¼″.

If you use 2x6 for G, apply glue to edge of G, screw G to C in position shown with 2¾″ No. 12 screws. Screw fence L to A with 2″ No. 10 screws.

Assemble drawers, Illus. 9. Screw J to K with 1½″ No. 10 screws. Apply glue and screw Q to J K with 1″ No. 8 screws. Fasten M in position, flush with top edge, with 1″ No. 8 screws.

Turn bench over and draw a center line on bottom of G, Illus. 14.

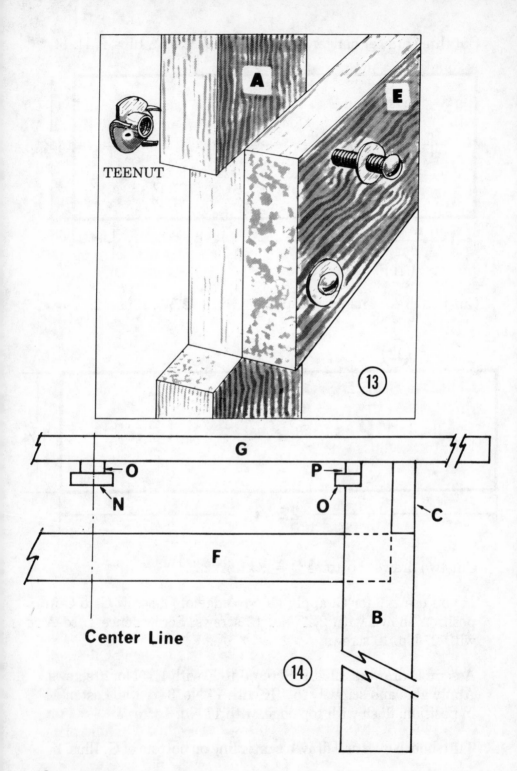

TEENUT

A

E

13

G

O

P

N

O

C

F

B

Center Line

14

Glue and nail O to N with 1″ brads. Drill holes and fasten O and N temporarily in position to G. Don't use glue.

Apply glue and nail O to P. Fasten O P in position shown to G with 2½″ No. 10 screws. Don't drive screws all the way. Install and test drawers. When drawers slide freely, apply glue, fasten O N and O P permanently in position.

If bench is to be subjected to heavy work, additional rigidity can be built into it by adding 1x3 diagonal braces from back of E to front of A. A 4x9″ woodworker's vise can be fastened to left front end of completed bench. Apply drawer pulls to drawers. Countersink all screw heads and fill holes with wood filler.

CHILD'S SIZE BENCH
LIST OF MATERIALS
1 pc. 2 x 3 x 10 ft. for R, S   or use 2 x 4
1 pc. 1 x 4 x 6 ft. for U
1 pc. 1 x 4 x 8 ft. for T, X   } Cut 1x4 to 1x3
1 pc. ¾ x 26 x 31″ Plywood for V, W
Eight ⅜ x 3″ Carriage Bolts, Washers and Nuts†
Forty-two 1¾″ No. 9 screws

† or Eight ⅜″ x 2½″ Cap Screws or Round Head
   Stove bolts, and Eight ⅜″ Teenuts.

While this list of materials permits building a child's size bench, Illus. 15, measuring 31″ long, 14″ deep, with bench top approximately 25¾″ from floor, legs can be cut any height desired. Since a growing child will use a workbench for years, we suggest building to height specified, even if it requires building a platform to stand on. The platform can be built with two 2x4 on edge, plus a ¾″ top, Illus. 16. This will raise child 4″. Build platform approximately 2′x3′ or size desired.

Cut all parts of bench to size indicated, Illus. 15, 17, 18. Notch R and S to receive T. When assembling, glue all permanent wood-to-wood contacts. Screw T to R and S. Bore ⅜" holes and bolt U to R and S. Screw V to T. Screw W to T and U. Screw X to S. If desired, drawers can be added by following procedure used for adult size bench. If drawers are to be installed, fasten Front Rail U 5" down from top of Leg R. Build drawers to fit smaller bench.

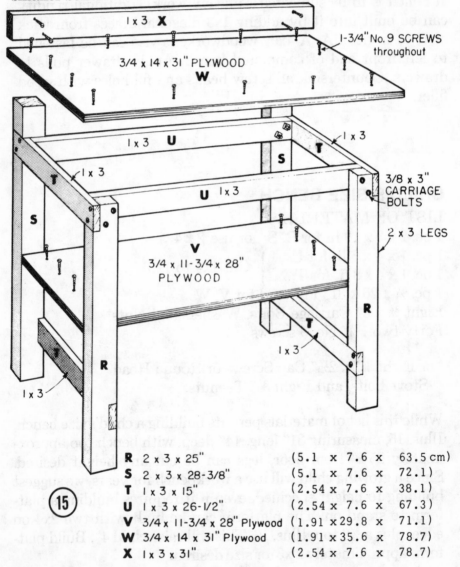

1 x 3 **X**

1-3/4" No. 9 SCREWS throughout

3/4 x 14 x 31" PLYWOOD
W

1 x 3 **U**

1 x 3

1 x 3
S
T

3/8 x 3"
CARRIAGE
BOLTS

U 1 x 3

1 x 3

2 x 3 LEGS

S

V
3/4 x 11-3/4 x 28"
PLYWOOD

R

1 x 3
R

T

1 x 3

1 x 3

(15)

R	2 x 3 x 25"	(5.1	x 7.6 x 63.5 cm)
S	2 x 3 x 28-3/8"	(5.1	x 7.6 x 72.1)
T	1 x 3 x 15"	(2.54	x 7.6 x 38.1)
U	1 x 3 x 26-1/2"	(2.54	x 7.6 x 67.3)
V	3/4 x 11-3/4 x 28" Plywood	(1.91	x 29.8 x 71.1)
W	3/4 x 14 x 31" Plywood	(1.91	x 35.6 x 78.7)
X	1 x 3 x 31"	(2.54	x 7.6 x 78.7)

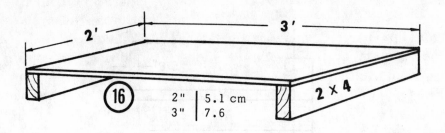

2'   3'

(16)

| 2" | 5.1 cm |
| 3" | 7.6 |

2 X 4

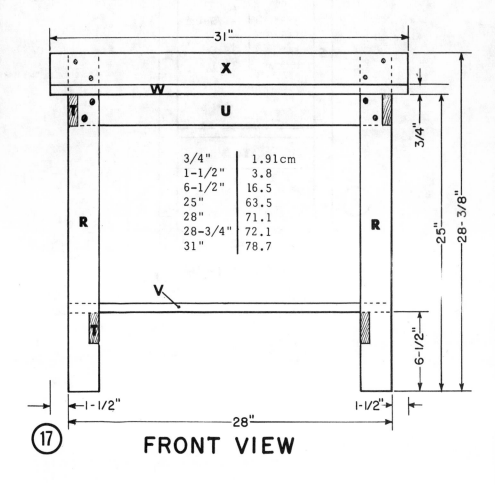

31"

X

W

T

U

3/4"

3/4"	1.91cm
1-1/2"	3.8
6-1/2"	16.5
25"	63.5
28"	71.1
28-3/4"	72.1
31"	78.7

R   R

28-3/8"

25"

V

T

6-1/2"

|—1-1/2"   1-1/2"—|

(17)

28"

FRONT VIEW

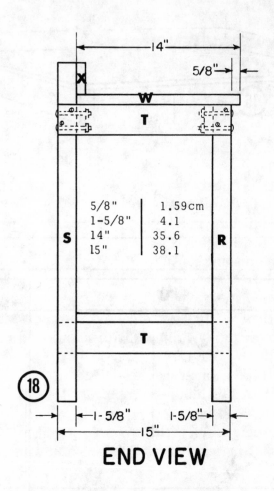

5/8"	1.59cm
1-5/8"	4.1
14"	35.6
15"	38.1

END VIEW

FOLDAWAY WORKBENCH

LIST OF MATERIALS
1 x 6 — 2/8, 2/10
1 x 12 — 2/10
5/4 x 4 — 4/8, 1/12, 1/6
5/4 x 2 — 1/4
One 4 ft. x 8 ft. ⅛" pegboard
One 3 ft. x 4 ft. ⅛" hardboard
¼ lb. 8 penny finishing nails
½ lb. 6 penny finishing nails
2 lbs. 4 penny finishing nails
1 box ¾" brads
1 box ¾" wire nails
One 3 ft. length of ½" threaded steel rod, four nuts and washers
Four 2" x 2" loose pin butt hinges with screws
Four door pulls
Four plunger type cabinet catches
One 16" length of 1" Aluminum tubing
One 18" length ⅞" Dowel
Four 2" x 2" Angle Irons with screws
Two ½" x 3" Carriage Bolts with washers and wing nuts

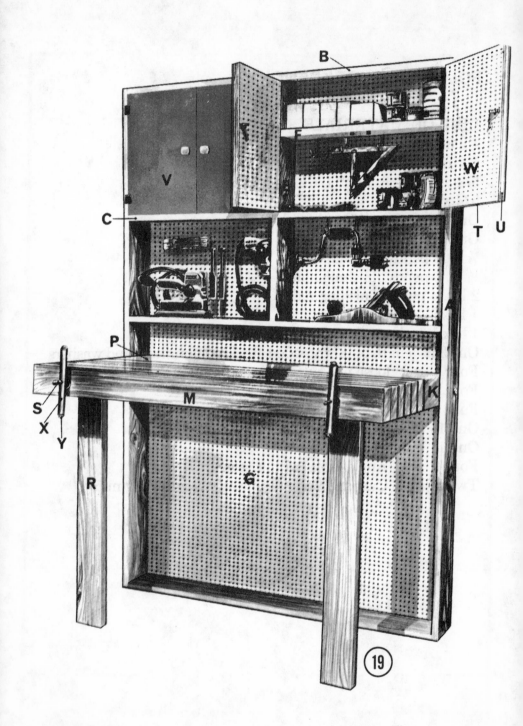

Cut two sides A-1x6x72″, Illus. 20. Bore ½″ holes where noted, Illus. 21, 31¾″ from floor for an adult size bench.

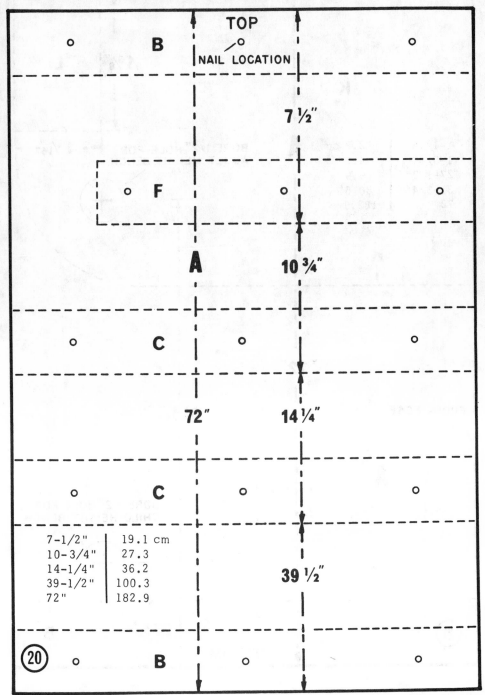

TOP

B

NAIL LOCATION

7 ½″

F

A

10 ¾″

C

72″

14 ¼″

C

7-1/2″	19.1 cm
10-3/4″	27.3
14-1/4″	36.2
39-1/2″	100.3
72″	182.9

39 ½″

20 B

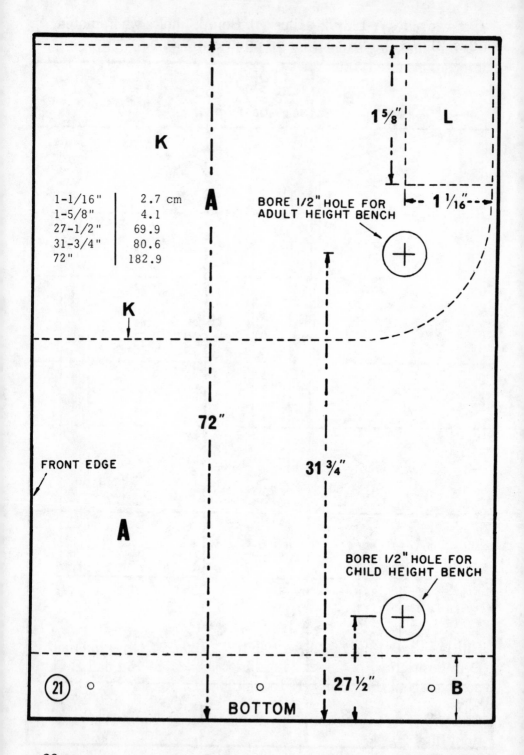

K

1⅝" L

1-1/16"	2.7 cm
1-5/8"	4.1
27-1/2"	69.9
31-3/4"	80.6
72"	182.9

A

BORE 1/2" HOLE FOR
ADULT HEIGHT BENCH

1 ¹⁄₁₆"

K

72"

31 ¾"

FRONT EDGE

A

BORE 1/2" HOLE FOR
CHILD HEIGHT BENCH

21   ○   ○   ○   27 ½"   ○   B

BOTTOM

Cut two B, two C — 1x6x46½". Apply glue and nail A to B with 6 penny finishing nails, Illus. 22. Glue and nail A to C Illus. 23, in position noted, Illus. 20

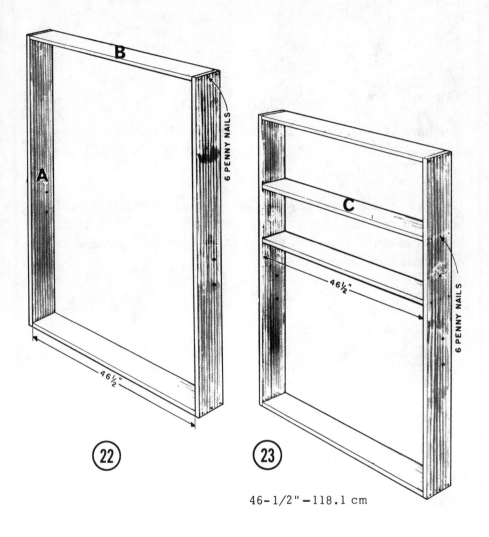

46-1/2" — 118.1 cm

Cut D — 1x6x13½"; cut E — 1x6x16¾", Illus. 24. Glue and nail D in position with 4 penny finishing nails. Glue and nail E in position. Nail thru B into E, toenail E to C.

Cut two F — 4-9/16"x22⅞" from 1x6. Glue and nail F in position, Illus. 20, 25.

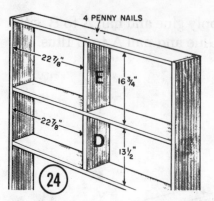

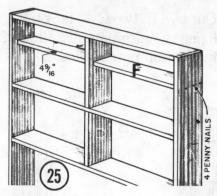

Cut back G — 4'0"x6'0/ from ⅛" pegboard, Illus. 26. Glue and nail G to A, B, C, D, E and F with 4 penny finishing nails spaced 10" to 12" apart.

Saw 1x2 in half and cut two H, two J, Illus. 27 to size indicated. Glue and nail HJ to back assembled unit, Illus. 28. HJ spaces back of assembled unit ¾" away from wall. This permits using pegboard tool holders in G.

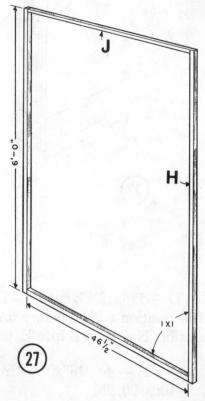

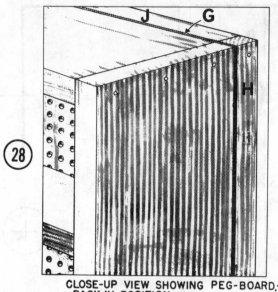

(28)

CLOSE-UP VIEW SHOWING PEG-BOARD,
BACK IN POSITION

Cut three K, Illus. 29, 3½x12⅞" from 5/4x4" lumber. Cut end to angle shown full size, Illus. 30. Drill ½" hole in position indicated. Cut one L from 5/4x2"x46⅜". Apply glue and assemble KLN with 8 penny finishing nails.

3-1/2"	8.9 cm
4-9/16"	11.6
13-1/2"	34.3
14"	35.6
16-3/4"	42.5
22-7/8"	58.1
46-3/8"	117.8
46-1/2"	118.1
4'	121.9
6'	182.9

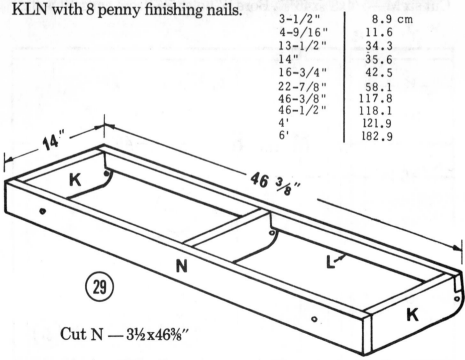

(29)

Cut N — 3½x46⅜"

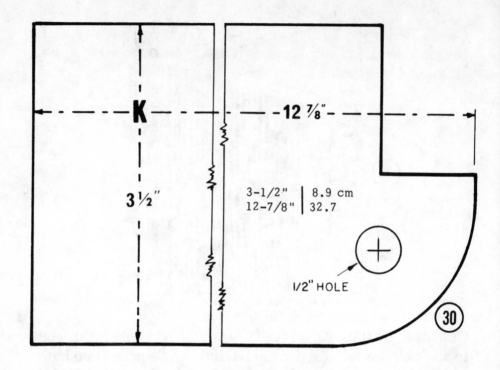

K

12 ⅞"

3 ½"

| 3-1/2" | 8.9 cm |
| 12-7/8" | 32.7 |

1/2" HOLE

(30)

Cut six M—5/4x3⅝x46⅜". Bore ½" holes 5½" from ends, Illus. 31.

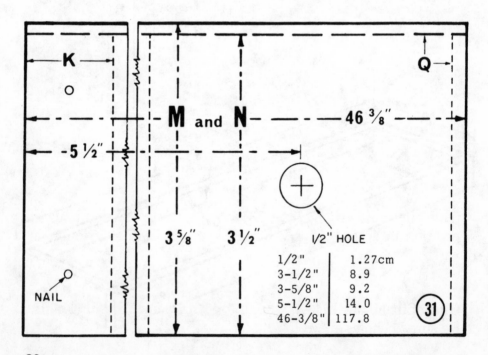

K

Q

M and N

46 ⅜"

5 ½"

3 ⅝"

3 ½"

1/2" HOLE

NAIL

1/2"	1.27cm
3-1/2"	8.9
3-5/8"	9.2
5-1/2"	14.0
46-3/8"	117.8

(31)

Cut ⅛″ tempered hardboard 14x46⅜″. Apply glue and nail P to assembled KLN with 4 penny finishing nails spaced 6″ apart, Illus. 32. Countersink heads, fill holes with wood filler.

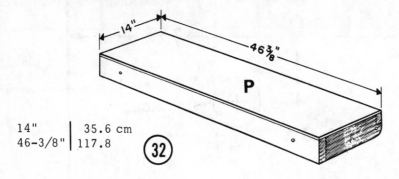

14"	35.6 cm
46-3/8"	117.8

Cut eight Q, Illus. 33, to size shown, Illus. 34. Use 5/4x4. Bore ½″ hole in position indicated.

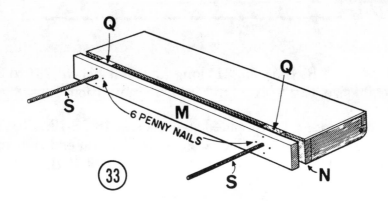

Glue and nail Q to N, Illus. 33, with 6 penny finishing nails in position indicated, Illus. 34. Nail Q in position so grain runs vertically.

Glue and nail one M to Q, Illus. 33, with 6 penny finishing nails. Be sure ½″ holes are in line.

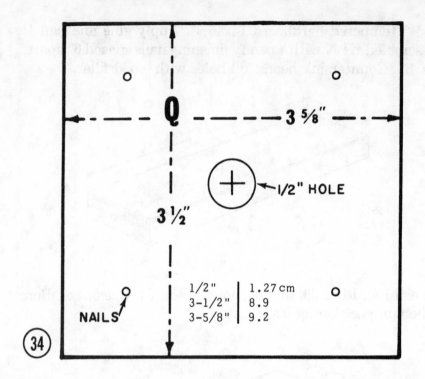

Q --- 3 ⅝"

3 ½"

+ ← 1/2" HOLE

1/2"	1.27 cm
3-1/2"	8.9
3-5/8"	9.2

NAILS

(34)

Cut two legs R, Illus. 35. 34" long for adult bench; 26" to 30" for child size. Use 5/4x4. Drill ½" hole in position, Illus. 36.

Cut two pieces of ½" threaded steel rods — 18", S-Illus. 33. Insert in position shown. Place washer and nut on end that projects thru N. Tighten nut so rod projects about 1" thru N.

Glue and nail other Q to M in position shown, Illus. 36. Place leg R in position on right hand rod. Do not use glue or nail as leg must swing freely on rod.

Glue and nail Q to M on left hand rod, Illus. 36. Place M in position on rods; glue and nail M to Q. Place leg R on left hand rod. Glue and nail Q to M on right hand rod. Place M in position. Glue and nail M to Q.

Place remaining M in position on S. Do not glue or nail this M in place as it acts as a vise. Illus. 37 shows bench top at this stage of construction.

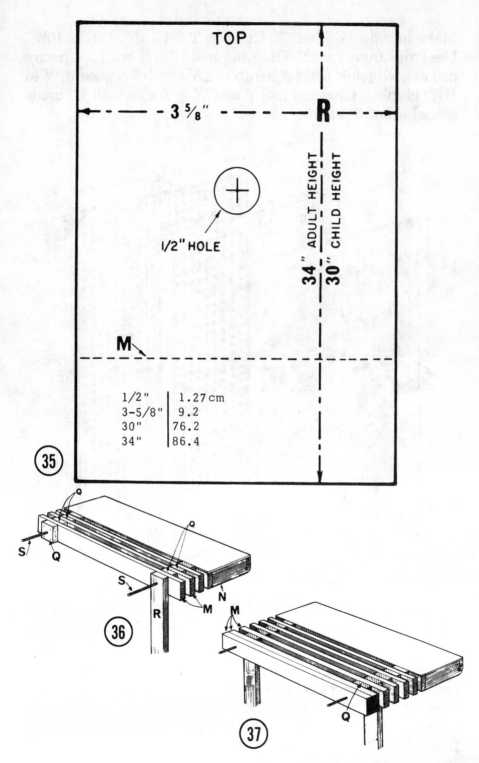

TOP

← 3 5/8" →

R

+

1/2" HOLE

34" ADULT HEIGHT
30" CHILD HEIGHT

M

1/2"	1.27 cm
3-5/8"	9.2
30"	76.2
34"	86.4

(35)

(36)

(37)

Make four doors, Illus. 38. Cut two T 9-15/16", two U 16¾".
Use strips from 1 x 12". Glue and nail U to T with a 4 penny
nail at each joint. Cut ⅛" hardboard V and ⅛" pegboard W to
11-7/16x16¾". Glue and nail V and W to frame with ¾" brads
spaced about 6" apart.

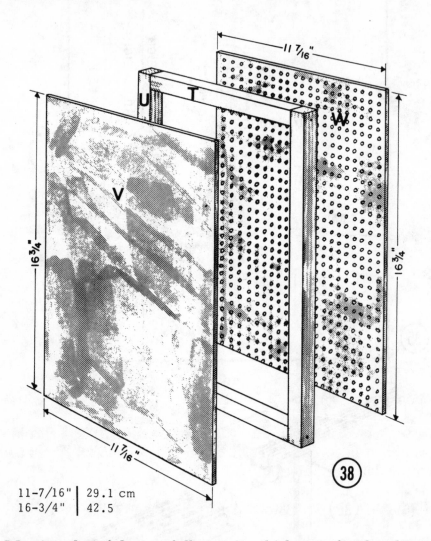

| 11-7/16" | 29.1 cm |
| 16-3/4" | 42.5 |

Mortise edge of door to fully receive thickness of a closed 2x2"
hinge. Bore hole to receive screw for door pull. Hang doors,
Illus. 19, with 2x2" loose pin butt hinges. If necessary, plane or
sandpaper doors to fit. Fasten 1" door pulls in position indicated,
Illus. 39.

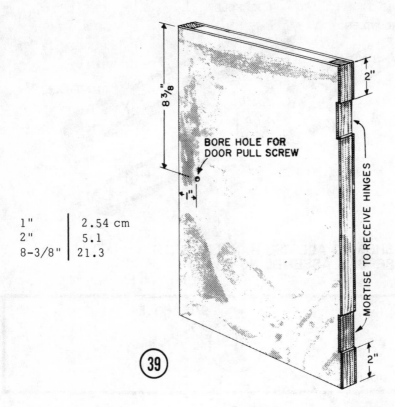

8 3/8"

BORE HOLE FOR
DOOR PULL SCREW

1"

2"

MORTISE TO RECEIVE HINGES

2"

39

1"	2.54 cm
2"	5.1
8-3/8"	21.3

Before completing assembly, paint workbench. Remove Vise M, legs R by removing bolts S. Countersink all nailheads, fill holes with wood filler.

Sandpaper all surfaces smooth.

We don't recommend painting benchtop or legs. These should be finished in 2 coats of Spar Varnish. Use colorful colors in painting balance of bench.

After painting, install cabinet catches to doors and bottom of F.

Make two vise handles, Illus. 40. Cut 1" aluminum tubing X, 8", Illus. 41. Bore $\frac{9}{16}$" through where indicated. Bore $\frac{1}{32}$" holes where indicated. Cut $\frac{7}{8}$" dowel Y, 8¾", Illus. 42. Round ends with file and sandpaper. Bore $\frac{9}{16}$" hole thru center. Saw Y in half and notch each part to receive nut Z, Illus. 40.

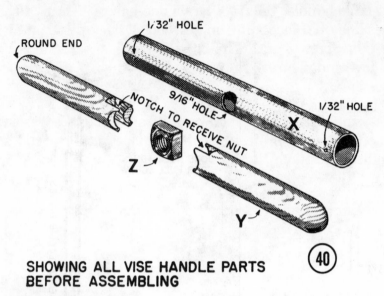

ROUND END

1/32" HOLE

9/16" HOLE

NOTCH TO RECEIVE NUT

1/32" HOLE

X

Z

Y

SHOWING ALL VISE HANDLE PARTS BEFORE ASSEMBLING

40

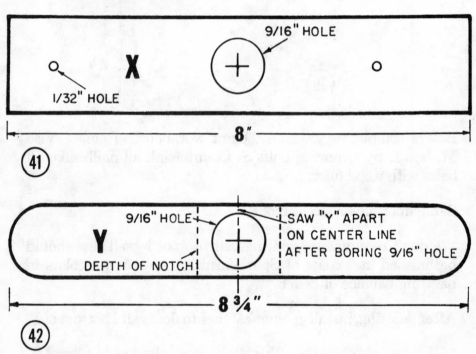

9/16" HOLE

X

1/32" HOLE

o

8"

41

9/16" HOLE

Y

DEPTH OF NOTCH

SAW "Y" APART
ON CENTER LINE
AFTER BORING 9/16" HOLE

8 ¾"

42

1/32"	.08 cm
9/16"	1.43
8-3/4"	22.2

36

Assemble handle, Illus. 43. Drive one-half of Y into X so $\frac{9}{16}''$ holes line up. Place nut Z in position. Drive other half of Y in position. Screw Z onto S to make certain it's locked in position. Remove and secure Y in position by driving $\frac{3}{4}''$ wire nails thru holes in X.

Reassemble benchtop as shown in Illus. 37. Replace washer and nut on end of rod projecting thru N. Place washer on rod, screw handle in position, Illus. 43.

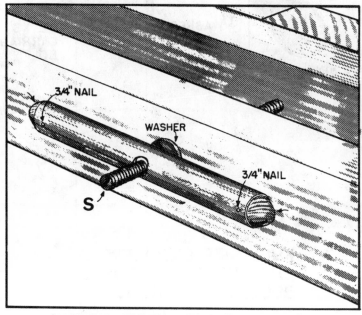

SHOWING ASSEMBLED VISE HANDLE IN POSITION ON BENCH

When vise is not in use, the projecting length of rod can be recessed by loosening handle and taking up on back nut.

Assemble benchtop by bolting K to A, Illus. 44, with $\frac{1}{2}$x3″ carriage bolt and wing nut.

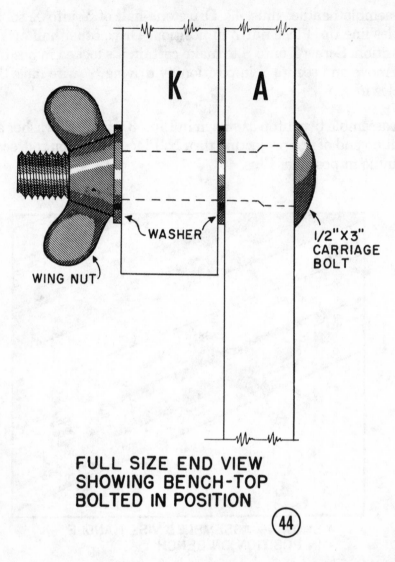

K **A**

WASHER

WING NUT

1/2"X3"
CARRIAGE
BOLT

FULL SIZE END VIEW
SHOWING BENCH-TOP
BOLTED IN POSITION

(44)

Place assembled unit in position with legs standing on level floor. Fasten A to wall with 2x2″ angle irons, Illus. 45.

NOTE: Best working height naturally varies with height of person using bench. We located benchtop at a comfortable average working height. If you are exceptionally tall or short, raise or lower benchtop. Before boring ½″ hole through A or cutting R to length, determine height suited to your requirements. Cut legs and bore ½″ holes through A where required.

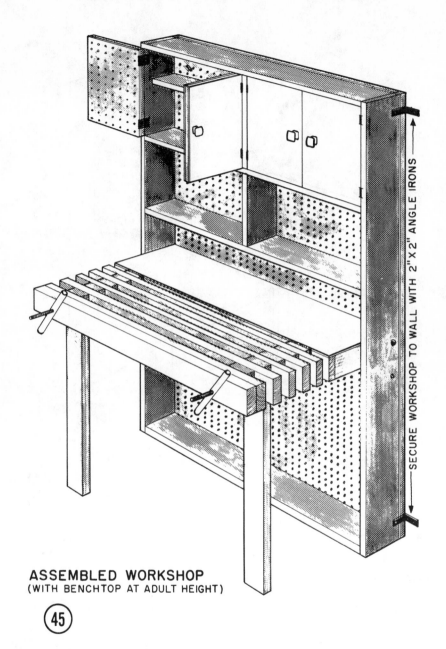

ASSEMBLED WORKSHOP
(WITH BENCHTOP AT ADULT HEIGHT)

(45)

This workshop can be used in many ways. To insert a large panel, Illus. 46, for use as a Sewing Center or Train Table, follow this construction procedure. Cut ¾" plywood panel 40"x6 ft. Panel can be cut larger or smaller if desired, but size specified is suitable for most uses. Notch panel as illustrated so it fits A.

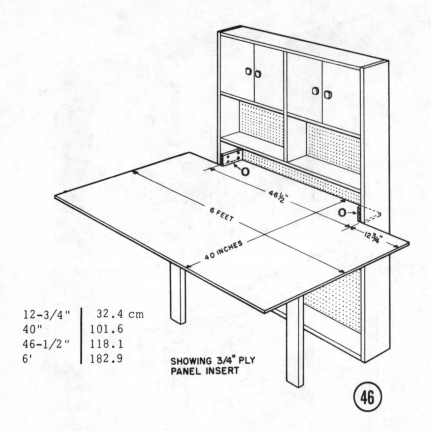

12-3/4"	32.4 cm
40"	101.6
46-1/2"	118.1
6'	182.9

SHOWING 3/4" PLY
PANEL INSERT

(46)

Cut two cleats "O" 5½" long from 5/4x4, Illus. 46. Temporarily clamp panel in position to benchtop. Apply glue and nail O to A with a few 4 penny nails, keeping bottom edge of O tight against panel. Carefully remove panel from its clamped position. Screw each O to A with four 1¾" No. 10 flathead wood screws. Cleats "O" prevent back of panel from swinging up when panel is slid in position.

To put workshop in foldaway position, loosen vise, swing legs up into slotted top, tighten vise, swing benchtop down. The slotted workbench top shown in Illus. 47, has many advantages. Cut two 6" long wedges from 5/4" stock. Material can be held tight in workbench as illustrated.

Another advantage of the slotted top is that shavings, sawdust, etc. will drop through to floor keeping working surface clear.

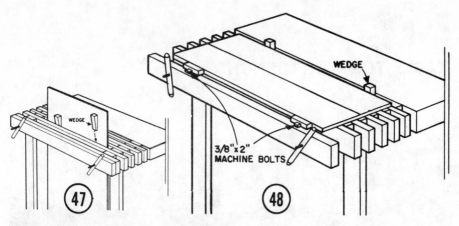

Benchtop can also be used as a clamp for gluing boards together, etc., as shown in Illus. 48. Bore ⅜″ holes 2″ deep in top edge of vise M. Drop ⅜x2″ machine bolts in holes. Head of machine bolt acts as bench "dog". Wedges hold edge of board. When vise is tightened, boards press together.

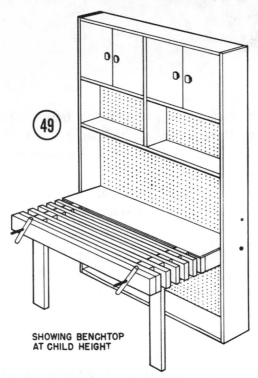

SHOWING BENCHTOP
AT CHILD HEIGHT

Countersink all screws. Fill holes with wood filler. To make an excellent filler, mix sawdust with glue.

TABLE TOP WORKBENCH

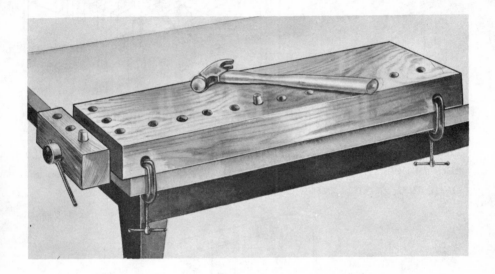

Need a workbench fast. Clamp this handy bench to any table and you have everything you need, including a vise. It provides the answer to the problem of where to make repairs. An ingenious peg system permits using the vise as a clamp to hold lumber and plywood up to 2 ft. wide. Measuring approximately 7" by 28" this bench can easily be stored in a drawer when not in use.

Before starting, read directions through carefully and note location of each part in each illustration. For greater strength and rigidity, glue all permanent joints. Maintain pressure on glued joints with weights or clamps until glue sets thoroughly. Wipe away excess glue with a damp rag before it sets.

Due to variance in lumber thickness, check size of parts against actual construction before cutting. Cut notches to fit your lumber.

LIST OF MATERIALS

1 — 5/4 x 2' x 2' oak for A, B, L
1 — 5/4 x 6 x 30" pine for C
1 — 1 x 3 x 5' pine for D
1 — 3/16" or ¼" x 8" x 30" tempered hardboard or plywood for E, F
1 — 2 x 3 x 8" oak for G
6 — 1¾" No. 10 flathead wood screws
12 — 1¼" No. 10 flathead wood screws
1 box ¾" brads
2 — 2" (open size) "C" clamps
1 — ½" x 9⅛" steel threaded rod, nut & washer for K
4" — ¾" dowel for N
½" x 17" steel rod for H unthreaded
¼" x 6" steel rod for M

Cut two A — 5/4 x 1½ x 5½, Illus. 50. Bore 3/16" holes through A where indicated.

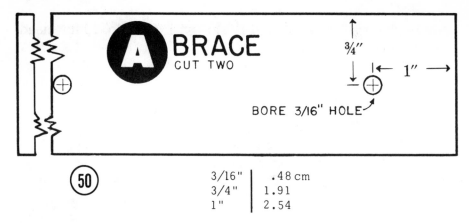

3/16"	.48 cm
3/4"	1.91
1"	2.54

Cut NUT BLOCK B same size, Illus. 51. Bore 3/16" holes through B where indicated. Mortise shaded area 1" deep to overall size a ½" nut for a threaded bolt requires. To mortise, first bore ⅜" holes 1" deep in position indicated, then cut holes square using a ¼" or ⅜" chisel. Insert nut in cutout.

43

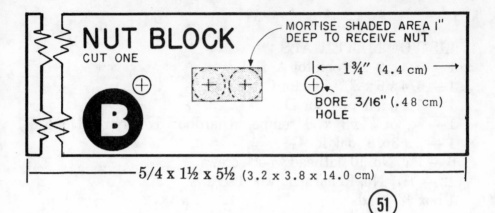

NUT BLOCK
CUT ONE

B

MORTISE SHADED AREA 1" DEEP TO RECEIVE NUT

⊕← 1¾" (4.4 cm) →

BORE 3/16" (.48 cm) HOLE

5/4 x 1½ x 5½ (3.2 x 3.8 x 14.0 cm)

(51)

Cut C, Illus. 52, to size indicated from 5/4 x 6" pine.

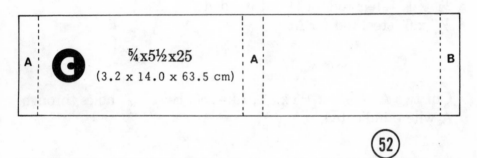

A   C   ⅝x5½x25
(3.2 x 14.0 x 63.5 cm)   A   B

(52)

Apply glue and fasten A and B to C with 1¾" No. 10 flat head wood screws, Illus. 53.

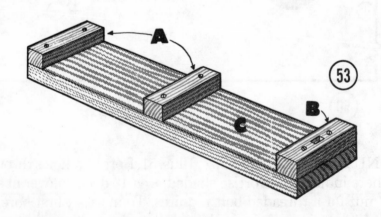

A

C

B

(53)

Cut two D, Illus. 54, to size indicated from 1 x 3 pine. Bore ¾″ holes 2″ from ends, in position shown.

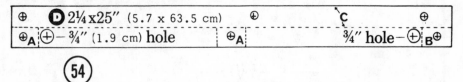

⊕   **◐ D** 2¼x25″ (5.7 x 63.5 cm)   ⊕   `C`   ⊕

⊕**A** ⊕– ¾″ (1.9 cm) hole   ⊕**A**   ¾″ hole–⊕ **B**⊕

(54)

Bore 3⁄16″ holes in position indicated, Illus. 55. Apply glue and fasten D to A, B and C with 1¼″ No. 10 flathead screws.

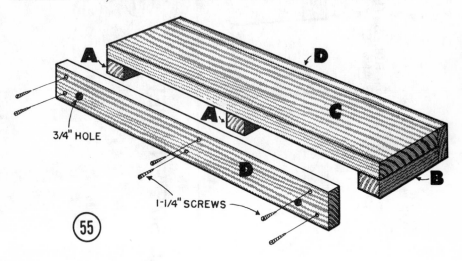

3/4" HOLE

1-1/4" SCREWS

(55)

Cut benchtop E to size shown, Illus. 56, from 3⁄16″ tempered hardboard or ¼″ plywood. Apply glue and nail E to C and D with ¾″ brads. Apply weight to bond E in place.

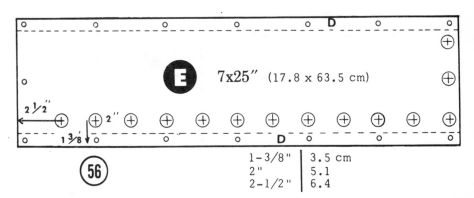

E 7x25″ (17.8 x 63.5 cm)

2½″

2″

1 3⁄8′

(56)

1–3/8″	3.5 cm
2″	5.1
2–1/2″	6.4

Bore ¾″ holes, 1″ deep at angle shown in full size end view, Illus. 57, in position shown in Illus. 58.

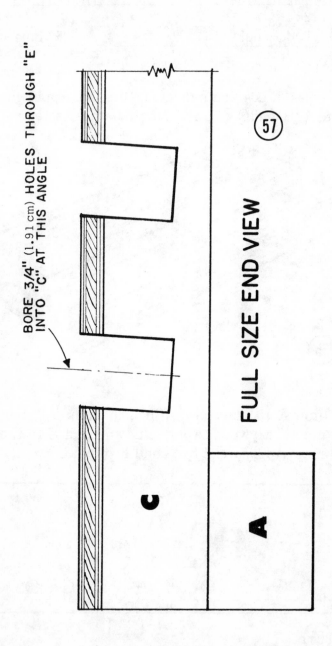

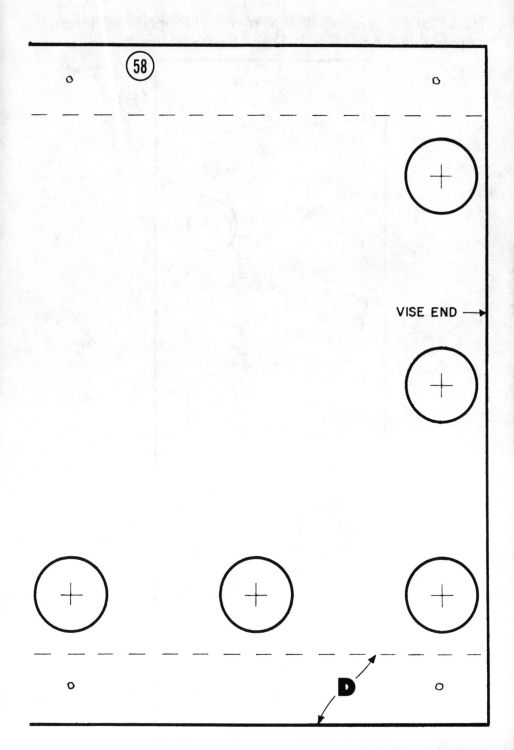

VISE END →

D

47

Cut F to size required, Illus. 59 from 3/16″ tempered hardboard. Apply glue and nail F to B, D and E with 3/4″ brads.

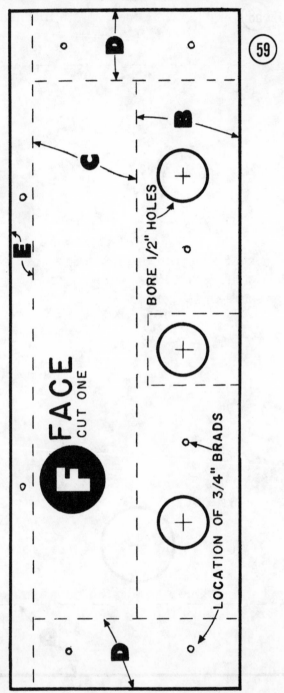

Using Illus. 59 as a template, drill ½″ holes through F and B. Use caution to drill holes straight and parallel to each other.

Illus. 60 shows assembled workbench up to this point.

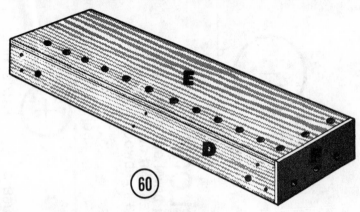

Cut Vise Block G, Illus. 61. Use a piece of 2 x 3 oak or other hardwood. To mark exact location of ½″ and ¾″ holes, and to drill these at exact angle required, do this.

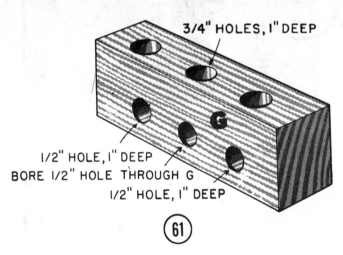

Cut Illus. 62 and 63 and glue together along line indicated so overall pattern looks like Illus. 64. Next, fold pattern down 90° along line indicated. Bore ¾″ holes, 1″ deep at angle indicated. Bore two ½″ holes, 1″ deep straight. Bore one ½″ hole through G where indicated, Illus. 62.

49

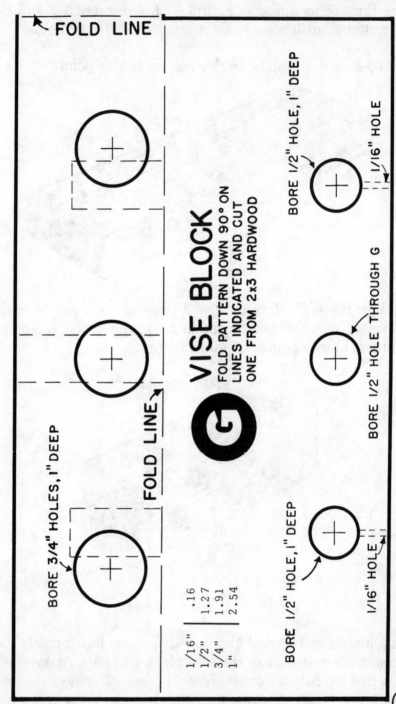

FOLD LINE

FOLD LINE

BORE 3/4" HOLES, 1" DEEP

BORE 1/2" HOLE, 1" DEEP

1/16" HOLE

BORE 1/2" HOLE THROUGH G

BORE 1/2" HOLE, 1" DEEP

1/16" HOLE

G VISE BLOCK

FOLD PATTERN DOWN 90° ON
LINES INDICATED AND CUT
ONE FROM 2x3 HARDWOOD

1/16"	.16
1/2"	1.27
3/4"	1.91
1"	2.54

62

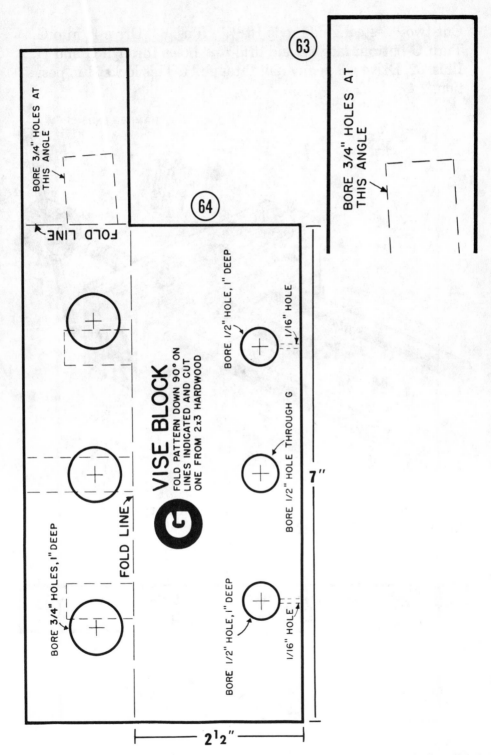

BORE 3/4" HOLES AT THIS ANGLE

63

BORE 3/4" HOLES AT THIS ANGLE

64

FOLD LINE

BORE 1/2" HOLE, 1" DEEP

1/16" HOLE

G VISE BLOCK
FOLD PATTERN DOWN 90° ON LINES INDICATED AND CUT ONE FROM 2x3 HARDWOOD

BORE 3/4" HOLES, 1" DEEP

FOLD LINE

BORE 1/2" HOLE THROUGH G

7"

BORE 1/2" HOLE, 1" DEEP

1/16" HOLE

2 1/2"

Cut two ½″ steel guide rods H 8¼″, Illus. 65. Drive H into G. Turn G bottom face up and drill $\frac{1}{16}$″ holes through G and H, Illus. 62. Drive a 3 penny nail through H. This locks H in position.

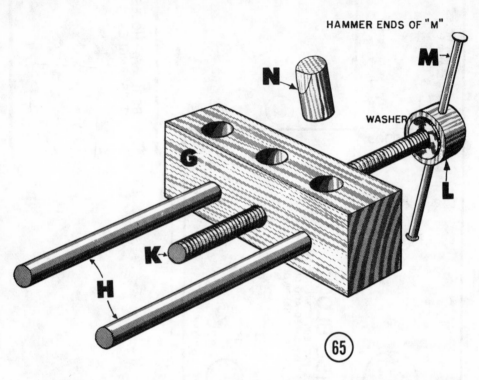

Cut a 9½″ vise screw K from ½″ threaded steel rod, Illus. 66. Bore ¼″ hole, ¼″ from end.

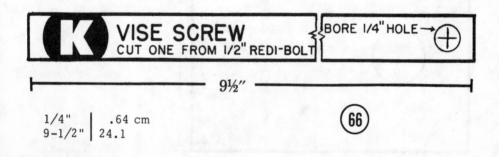

1/4"	.64 cm
9-1/2"	24.1

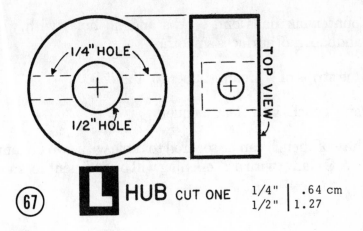

1/4" HOLE

1/2" HOLE

TOP VIEW

⑥⑦ **L** HUB CUT ONE 1/4" | .64 cm
                          1/2" | 1.27

Cut hub L Illus. 67, from 5/4 x 2″ oak. Bore a ½″ hole ⅝″ deep in center. Bore ¼″ hole through L in position shown.

Cut 6″ handle M, from ¼″ rod.

Place washer on K in position shown, Illus. 65.

Insert K in L. Line up hole in K with hole in L and insert M in position shown. Hammer both ends of M flat so it can't slide out.

Insert K through G. Place bench upside down on a flat surface. Place ½″ nut in B.

Insert H through F and B. Screw K into nut in B.

Cut two 1½″ lengths of ¾″ dowel, Illus. 68, for pegs N. If necessary, sandpaper N so it fits easily into ¾″ holes in E and G. If you sandpaper part of N flat as shown, it provides a better face when butting against boards.

⑥⑧ **N** PEG
CUT TWO
from 3/4" dowel

BEVEL

3/4" — 1.91 cm

Countersink nails and screws and fill holes with wood filler. Sandpaper all surfaces smooth.

Glue strips of ¼" foam rubber to A and B.

Paint bench with clear lacquer.

The workbench can be secured to table with two C clamps, Illus. 69. A C clamp with a 2" opening will be sufficient for most tables.

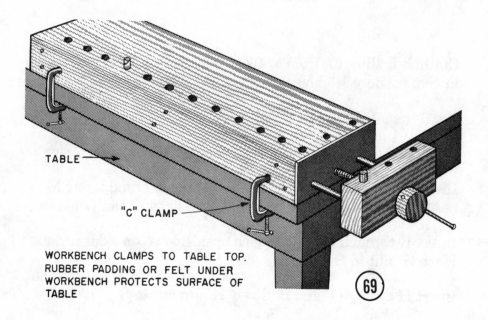

TABLE

"C" CLAMP

WORKBENCH CLAMPS TO TABLE TOP. RUBBER PADDING OR FELT UNDER WORKBENCH PROTECTS SURFACE OF TABLE

69

A self opening vise can be made by following optional construction shown in Illus. 70 to 74.

Cut two pieces of 1/16" thick flat steel — 1¼" x 1¼" for plate P. Bore and countersink ⅝" no 3 flathead wood screws, Illus. 70. Screw pieces in place on a scrap piece of wood. Bore ⅜" hole in center as shown.

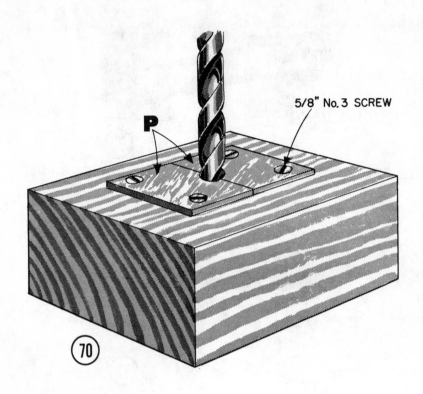

5/8" No. 3 SCREW

P

70

File a ⅛" wide slot ¹⁄₁₆" deep, ¾" from end of K, Illus. 71.

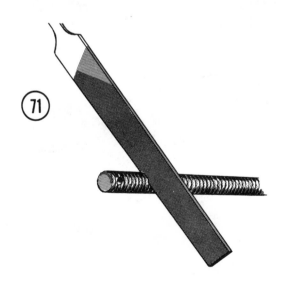

71

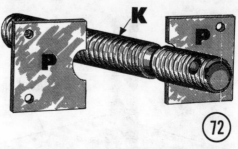

Illus. 72 and 73 show how pieces P fit around K.

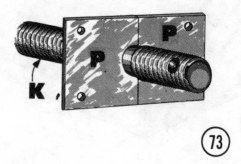

Slide K through G. Screw P in place around K, Illus. 74. Slip hub L over end of K. Line up ¼″ holes in L and K. Slide handle M in position through L and K. Hammer both ends of M flat so that M cannot slide out of assembled LK.

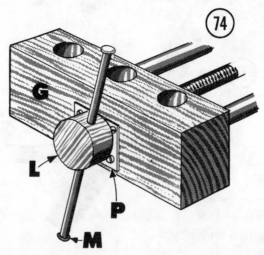

SAWHORSE TOOL CHEST

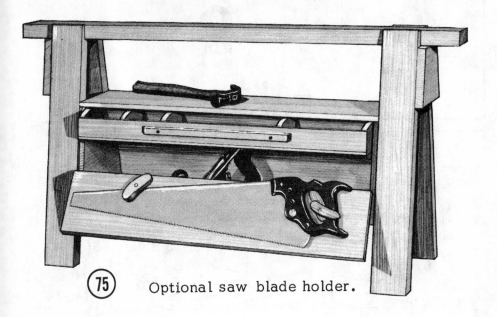

(75) Optional saw blade holder.

MATERIALS NEEDED
1 — 2x4x14' — A, B
1 — ½"x4'x4' plywood for C, D, E, F,
    G, H, J, K, L, M, N, O, R
¼" plywood scraps for Q
¼ lb. 4, 6 and 10 penny finishing nails
1 pair butterfly hinges
3 — 1" No. 8 flathead wood screws
12 — ¾" No. 6 flathead wood screws
2 — 1¼" No. 8 flathead screws

Due to the variance in lumber width and thickness, after you start assembly, cut additional parts to size your project requires.

Cut one rail A — 2x4x47". Notch A in position shown, Illus. 76, 77. Cut notch to width 2x4 legs B require, Illus. 78.

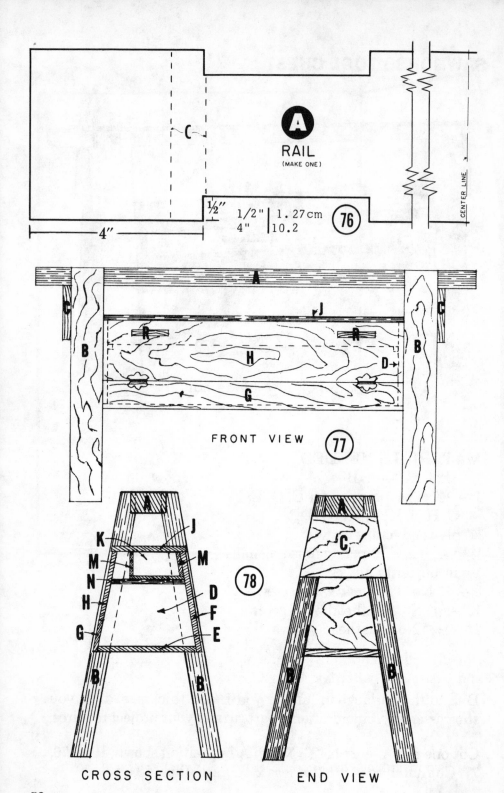

A

RAIL

(MAKE ONE)

| | 1/2" | 1.27 cm |
| 76 | 4" | 10.2 |

FRONT VIEW 77

78

CROSS SECTION   END VIEW

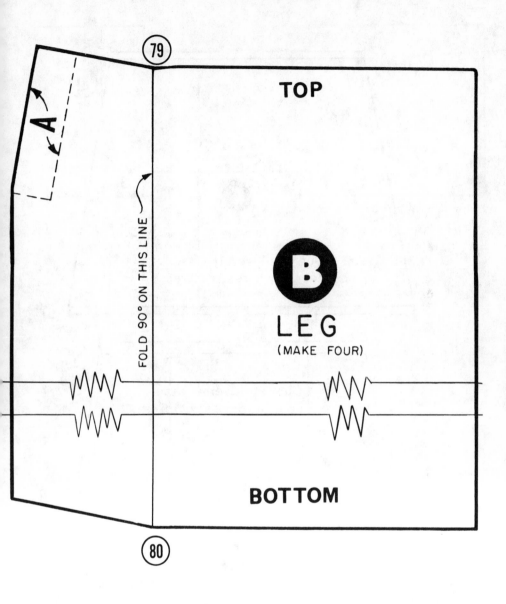

Cut four legs B — 2x4x24¼", or height you prefer. If you fold Illus. 79, 80 — 90° along line indicated, it shows angle to cut B, and position of notch for A.

Cut two outside cleats C from ½" plywood, to size shown in Illus. 81.

Cut two inside leg chest ends D from ½" plywood to size shown, Illus. 82.

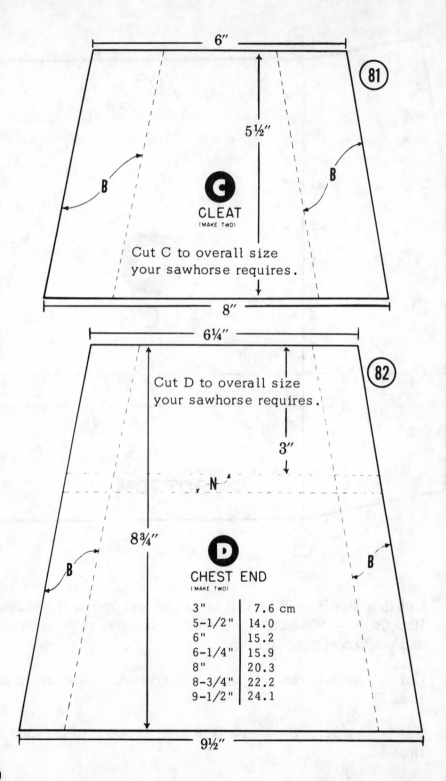

6″

(81)

5½″

C

CLEAT
(MAKE TWO)

Cut C to overall size
your sawhorse requires.

B

B

8″

6¼″

(82)

Cut D to overall size
your sawhorse requires.

3″

N

8¾″

D

CHEST END
(MAKE TWO)

3″	7.6 cm
5-1/2″	14.0
6″	15.2
6-1/4″	15.9
8″	20.3
8-3/4″	22.2
9-1/2″	24.1

B

B

9½″

Apply glue before fastening parts.

Nail B to A with 10d nails. Nail D to B with 6d nails. Nail C to B with 10d nails.

Cut one bottom E and back F — ½x9⅝x32″; one G — ½x3x32″; one lid H — ½x6¾x32″. Bevel edges of E, F and H as indicated, Illus. 83.

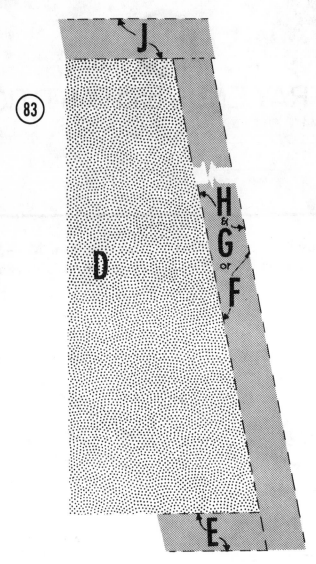

Cut top J — ½x7¼x32″. Bevel edges.

Nail E to D, F to D and E, G to D and E, J to D and F with 6d nails.

Cut 5 tray ends K from ½ plywood to size shown, Illus. 84.

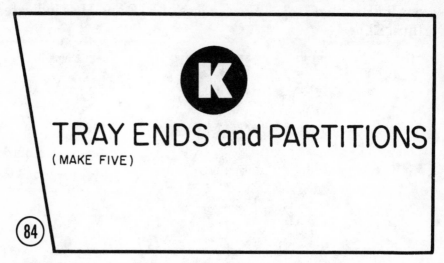

K

TRAY ENDS and PARTITIONS
(MAKE FIVE)

84

Cut one tray bottom L — ½x5⅜x30¾″; one front M — ½x2½x 30¾″; one back M — ½x2⅝x30¾″. Bevel edges, Illus. 85.

Nail front and back M to end K.

Nail L to K and M with 4d nails. Space other partitions K to suit your needs.

85

M

K

R

M

K

L

TRAY
CONSTRUCTION

Cut two tray slides N — ½x½x7½". Bevel ends to shape required, Illus. 86. Drill holes for No. 6 screws where indicated. Screw N to D with ¾" screws in position noted, Illus. 82.

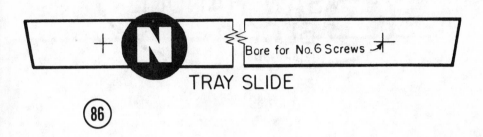

TRAY SLIDE

86

To mount a saw on inside face of H, make saw rack O, Illus. 87, for blade; and block P, Illus. 88, for handle. Cut two O — ½x¾x 6"; cut two spacers ¼x¾x¾.

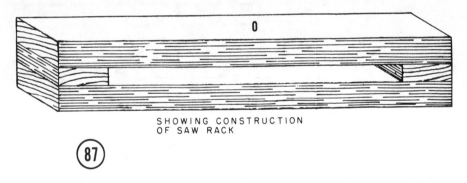

O

SHOWING CONSTRUCTION
OF SAW RACK

87

Cut block P to shape shown, Illus. 88, from 1" thick scrap. Cut one screw button Q to shape shown from ¼" scrap, Illus. 89. Screw P to inside face of H, in position saw requires with two 1" No. 8 screws. Screw Q to P with one ¾" No. 8 roundhead screw in center of P. Q rotates on P, Illus. 90.

Cut four tray and lid grips R, Illus. 85. Screw two to outside face of H about 3" from ends, about 1¼" down from top edge.

Hinge H to G with two butterfly hinges, Illus. 77.

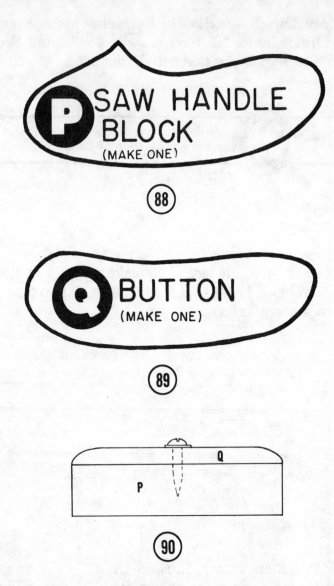

P SAW HANDLE BLOCK
(MAKE ONE)

88

Q BUTTON
(MAKE ONE)

89

Q

P

90

Now that you have a workbench, use it every time you need to make a repair, improvement, or to build whatever project your home requires. Pages 66 to 96 contain Easi-Bild Patterns that could help a child develop a lifelong interest in woodworking.

HOW TO THINK METRIC

Government officials concerned with the adoption of the metric system are quick to warn anyone from attempting to make precise conversions. One quickly accepts this advice when they begin to convert yards to meters or vice versa. Place a metric ruler alongside a foot ruler and you get the message fast.

Since a meter equals 1.09361 yards, or 39⅜"+, the decimals can drive you up a creek. The government men suggest accepting a rough, rather than an exact equivalent. They recommend considering a meter in the same way you presently use a yard. A kilometer as 0.6 of a mile. A kilogram or kilo as just over two pounds. A liter, a quart, with a small extra swig.

To more fully appreciate why a rough conversion is preferable, note the 6" rule alongside the metric rule. A meter contains 100 centimeters. A centimeter contains 10 millimeters.

As an introduction to the metric system, we used a metric rule to measure standard U.S. building materials. Since a 1x2 measures anywheres from ¾ to ²⁵⁄₃₂ x 1½", which is typical of U.S. lumber sizes, the metric equivalents shown are only approximate.

Consider 1" equal to 2.54 centimeters;
10" = 25.4 cm.
To multiply 4¼" into centimeters: $4.25 \times 2.54 = 10.795$ or 10.8 cm.

APPLIQUE SHELF

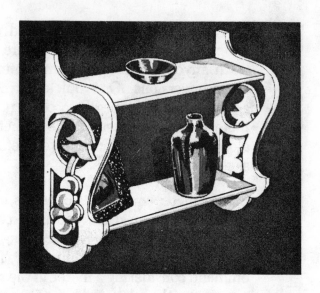

LIST OF MATERIALS
1 — ¼" x 17" x 18" hardwood or plywood
1 — ½" x 6" x 36" hardwood or plywood
⅜" brads, ten ¾" No. 6 screws, glue, paint

Solid outside lines indicate pattern. Dash lines show relative position of adjoining part. Pattern A is in 3 parts. Tape at X also at Y. Pattern B is in 2 parts. Connect at Z. Glue all wood-to-wood contacts.

Cut two sides A, two appliques B from ¼" hardwood or plywood. Cut two shelves C to width indicated on pattern by 18" long. Use ½" hardwood or plywood. Round front edge as shown.

Glue and brad B to A with ⅜" brads. Bore holes for No. 6 screws where indicated on pattern A. Apply glue and screw A to C with ¾" No. 6 flathead wood screws. Countersink heads of screws and brads. Fill holes with a wood filler.

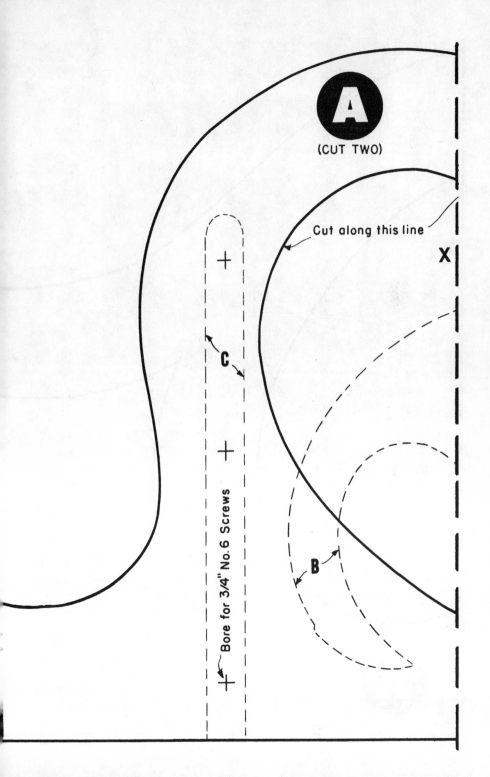

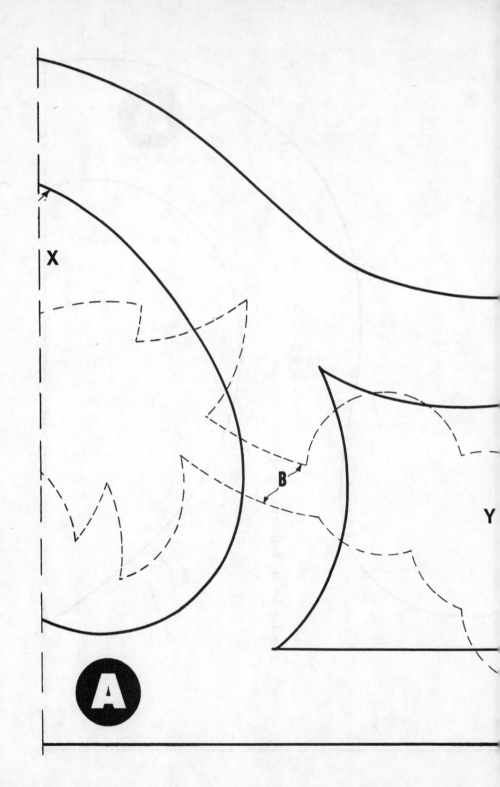

X

B

Y

A

Sand surfaces smooth. Paint project with a primer. When dry, paint parts with colors suggested.

Hang shelf to wall using two 1½″ angle irons fastened to studs in wall.

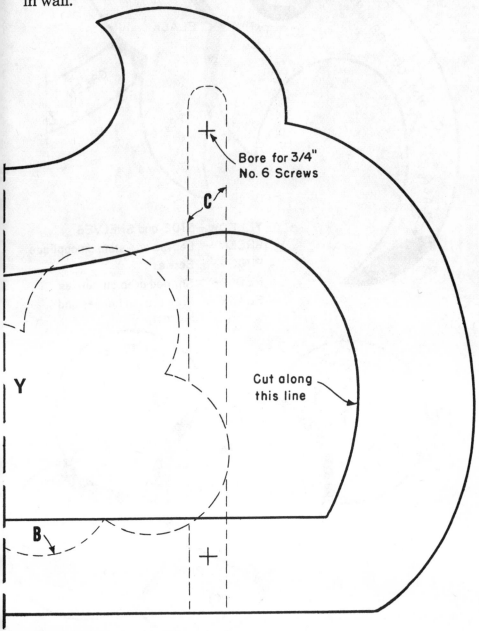

Bore for 3/4″
No. 6 Screws

C

Cut along
this line

Y

B

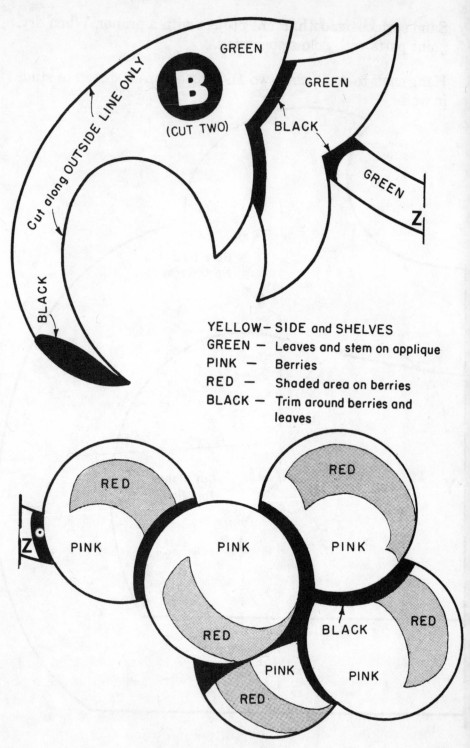

GREEN

GREEN

BLACK

B
(CUT TWO)

Cut along OUTSIDE LINE ONLY

GREEN

Z

BLACK

YELLOW— SIDE and SHELVES
GREEN — Leaves and stem on applique
PINK — Berries
RED — Shaded area on berries
BLACK — Trim around berries and leaves

RED

RED

Z

PINK

PINK

PINK

RED

BLACK

RED

PINK

PINK

RED

LAWN ORNAMENTS

LIST OF MATERIALS

1 — ¾" x 10" x 17" lumber or exterior grade plywood
1 — ½" x 4½" x 4½" exterior grade plywood
2 — ⅜" x 8" iron rods
1 — ¼" x 5"
Paint

COLOR GUIDE

YELLOW – DUCK, CHICK, Beak on Hen
WHITE – HEN, Eyeballs
RED – Comb and Wattle on Hen, Beaks on Duck and Chick
BLUE – Feather Outlines on Hen
BLACK – Chick and Duck Feather Outlines, Eyeballs,
Eye and Mouth Outlines

Solid black outside lines indicate pattern.

The Duck is full size in two parts. The Hen is full size in three parts. Connect Hen at Y and in position outline indicates.

Cut Hen and Duck from ¾" wood or exterior grade plywood. Bore hole for ⅜" iron rod in position indicated.

Cut Chick from ½" wood. Bore hole for ¼" iron rod where indicated.

Smooth edges with a file or sandpaper.

Paint edges as well as both surfaces with a primer.

Use carbon paper to trace outlines. Paint in colors suggested on color chart. Use exterior paint.

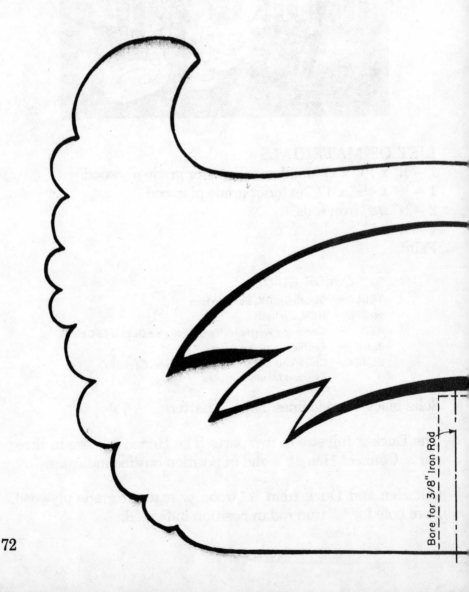

Bore for 3/8" Iron Rod

DUCK

Bore for
1/4" Iron Rod

CHICK

74

Insert ⅜″ x 8″ rod in Duck and Hen.

Insert ¼″ x 5″ rod in Chick. Press rods into ground to stand ornaments on lawn.

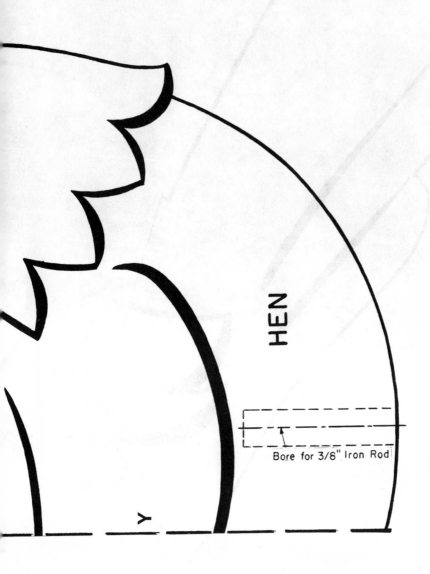

HEN

Y

Bore for 3/8″ Iron Rod

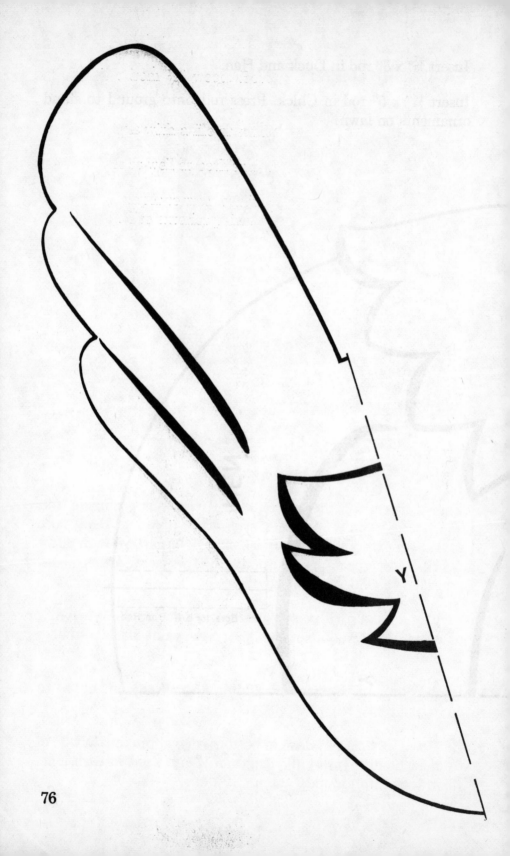

Y

LAWN ORNAMENT

LIST OF MATERIALS

1 — ½″ or ⅝″ x 9½″ x 15″ exterior grade plywood
2 — ¼″ x 10″ iron rods.

Tape pattern together. Then cut pattern along outside line. Trace outline on ½″ or ⅝″ exterior grade plywood. Paint both sides with exterior primer. Blacken back of pattern with a soft pencil. Attach pattern to cutout with tape. Using a sharp hard pencil trace all decorating guides.

Paint solid areas with color specified in color guide. When dry, paint dark blue polka dots on skirt. Next paint black trim lines on pattern.

Flesh color can be mixed by adding a small amount of red to white paint.

Bore two ¼″ holes, 2″ deep in bottom edge approximately 2″ in from each edge. Insert 10″ length of ¼″ iron rod in each hole. Press rods into ground.

COLOR GUIDE

FLESH – Face, Arms
YELLOW– Hair, Skirt
RED –   Hair Ribbon, Flower, Flower Pot
DK. BLUE – Polka Dots
GRAY – Sprinkling Can
BLACK – Shoes, Trim
GREEN – Grass, Leaves
WHITE – Socks, Blouse, Highlights on
              Shoes

Paint ornament in this sequence:
Face, arms, hair, skirt, hair ribbon,
flower, flower pot, blouse, socks,
shoe highlights, grass, leaves,
sprinkling can, polka dots, eye,
eyebrow, shoes, black outlines
and trim.

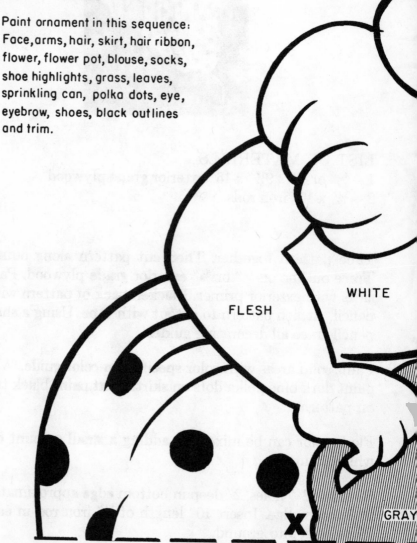

WHITE

FLESH

X

GRAY

YELLOW

RED

PONY PULL TOY AND PLANTER

LIST OF MATERIALS
1 — ¼″ x 7″ x 15″ plywood for A, B, C, D
1 — ⅜″ x 6″ x 12″ plywood for F, G, H
1 — ¾″ x ¾″ x 5½″ for E
1 — ¼″ x 1¼″ dowel
3 — ½″ #6 flathead wood screws
2 — ¾″ #6 flathead wood screws
2 — 1″ #8 roundhead wood screws and washers

All patterns are full size. Apply glue before nailing parts together.

Cut one A, two B. Plane edge of A and B to angle indicated. Cut two C. Glue and nail B to A with ¾″ brads. Glue and nail C to A and B. Cut one D from ¼″ plywood. Cut one axle E from 1″ lumber. Notch E to receive D. Cut two wheels F from ⅜″ plywood. Bore hole to receive No. 8 roundhead wood screw.

Fasten D in position to A with three ½″ #6 flathead wood screws. Fasten A to E with two ¾″ #6 flathead screws.

Cut pony G from ⅜" plywood. Bore hole for ¼" dowel. Hole must be sufficient size to allow dowel to turn freely.

Cut two wheels H from ⅜" plywood. Bore hole so ¼" dowel fits tight in wheel.

Countersink nails. Fill holes with wood filler. Sand surfaces smooth. Round sharp edges with sandpaper. Prime coat all parts using a white primer.

Trace decorating guides on pony. Paint all pieces using colors suggested. When paint has dried, insert washer between end of E and F and fasten F to E with a 1" #8 roundhead wood screw. Allow wheel F to turn freely on screw.

Cut ¼" dowel 1¼". Glue one end to H. Insert dowel through G. Glue other end of dowel to H. Nail D to G with ¾" brads.

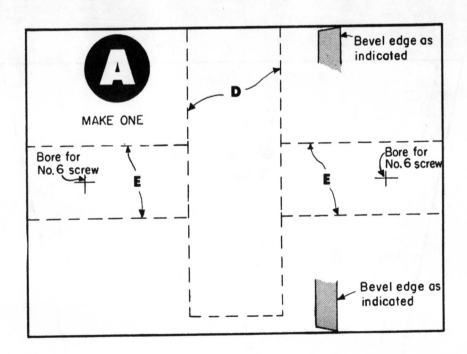

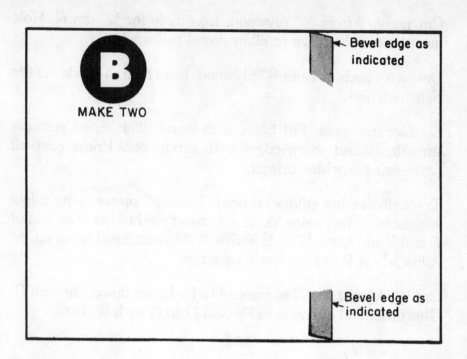

B

MAKE TWO

Bevel edge as indicated

Bevel edge as indicated

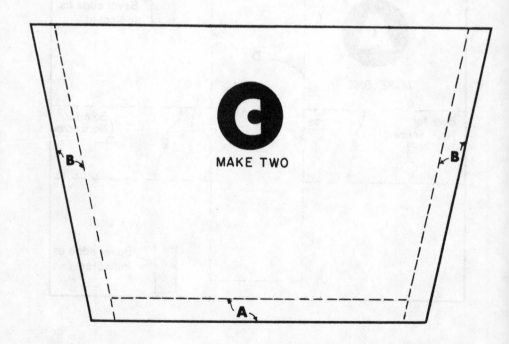

C

MAKE TWO

B

B

A

84

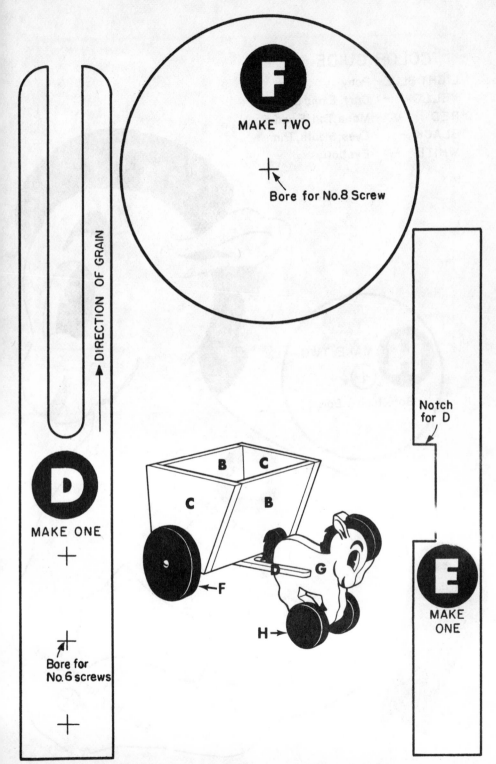

F

MAKE TWO

Bore for No.8 Screw

DIRECTION OF GRAIN

D

MAKE ONE

Bore for No.6 screws

Notch for D

E

MAKE ONE

B C

C B

F

D G

H

COLOR GUIDE

LIGHT BLUE – Pony
YELLOW   – Cart, E and D
RED   – Mane, Tail, F and H
BLACK   – Eyes, Mouth, Trim
WHITE   – Eyeball

H MAKE TWO
Bore for 1/4" Dowel

G MAKE ONE

D

Bore hole for 1/4" Dowel

DOOR STOPS

 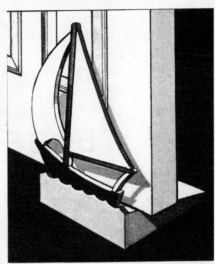

LIST OF MATERIALS
1 — ⅜″ x 5″ x 7¼″ plywood
1 — 5/4″ x 5″ x 5″
3 — 1″ #8 flathead screws

RABBIT. Cut pattern along solid outside line. Trace pattern on ⅜″ plywood and saw along outline.

Cut one base from 5/4″ x 4½″ x 5″. Taper base to shape indicated in End View.

Apply glue and fasten rabbit to base with three 1″ #8 flathead screws in position pattern indicates. Countersink screw heads. Fill holes with a wood filler. Sandpaper project smooth. Apply a primer coat. When dry trace outlines and paint colors in position indicated.

SAILBOAT. Cut out shaded area. Trace pattern on ⅜″ plywood. Follow same step-by-step construction as outlined above.

BASE
(MAKE ONE)

Direction of Grain

END VIEW OF BASE

TAPER OFF SHADED AREA

COLOR GUIDE
RABBIT
GREEN – BASE
PINK – BODY
BLACK – TRIM
WHITE – EYEBALL, TEETH

BLACK

PINK

Bore for 1"No.8 Screws

GREEN

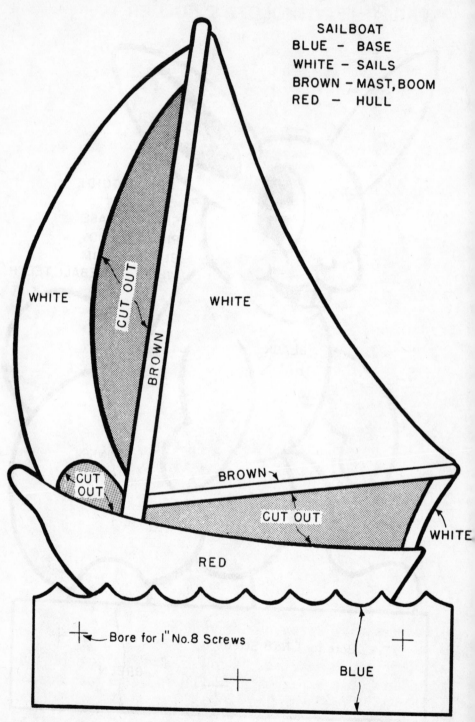

SAILBOAT
BLUE – BASE
WHITE – SAILS
BROWN – MAST, BOOM
RED – HULL

CUT OUT

BROWN

WHITE

WHITE

CUT OUT

BROWN

CUT OUT

WHITE

RED

Bore for 1" No.8 Screws

BLUE

90

PIERRE THE POTHOLDER'S HOLDER

LIST OF MATERIALS
1 — ⅜" x 10" x 20" plywood
8 — ¾" #6 screws
2 — 1½" #8 screws
2 — 10 penny nails

Solid outside line indicates pattern. Long dash line (− − − −) indicates where to recut pattern for C.

Short Dash lines (- - - - - - - - -) indicates location of adjoining parts. Apply glue before fastening parts together. Use ⅜" plywood for A, B and C.

Cut Chef A. Cut one full circle for B. Bore 7 holes for #6 screws, two holes for #8 screws in position indicated.

Pattern C is one half. Cut C to full size. Notch C to depth indicated to receive A. Apply glue and fasten B to A with three ¾" #6 screws; B to C with four ¾" #6 screws; C to A with one ¾" #6 screw.

Bore hole in bottom of each leg to receive and hold a 10-penny nail. Bend nails as shown before driving in position. These bent nail "feet" serve as hangers for potholders.

Sand all surfaces and edges smooth. Apply coat of primer. Using carbon paper, trace decorating guides on Chef onto project. Paint A, B and C colors suggested in painting guide. Shelf can be used to hold salt and pepper shakers, spices, a clock, etc.

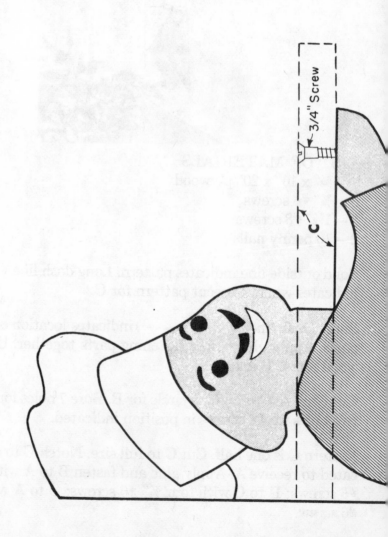

COLOR GUIDE

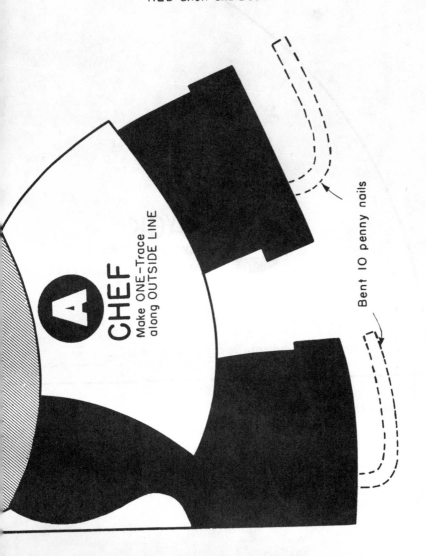

■ BLUE

▨ YELLOW

▧ FLESH

WHITE Apron, Hat, Teeth

BLACK Eyes, Eyebrows, Mustache
and Outlines

RED Shelf and Back

CHEF

Make ONE—Trace
along OUTSIDE LINE

Bent 10 penny nails

A

93

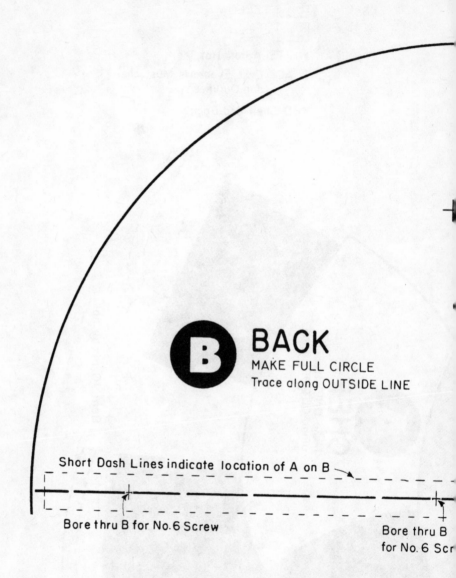

B BACK
MAKE FULL CIRCLE
Trace along OUTSIDE LINE

Short Dash Lines indicate location of A on B

Bore thru B for No. 6 Screw

Bore thru B
for No. 6 Scr

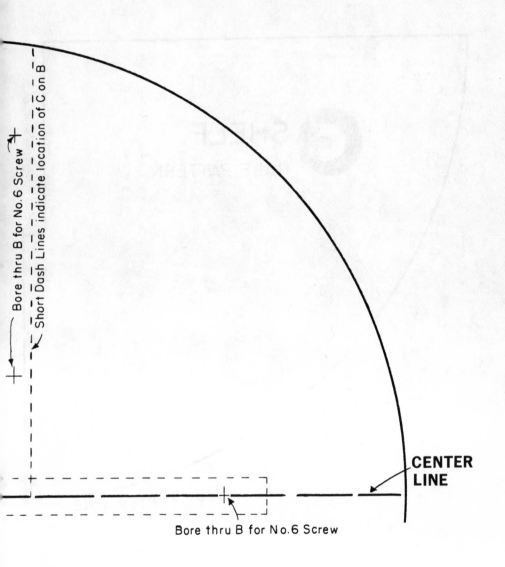

Bore thru B for No. 6 Screw

Short Dash Lines indicate location of C on B

CENTER LINE

Bore thru B for No.6 Screw

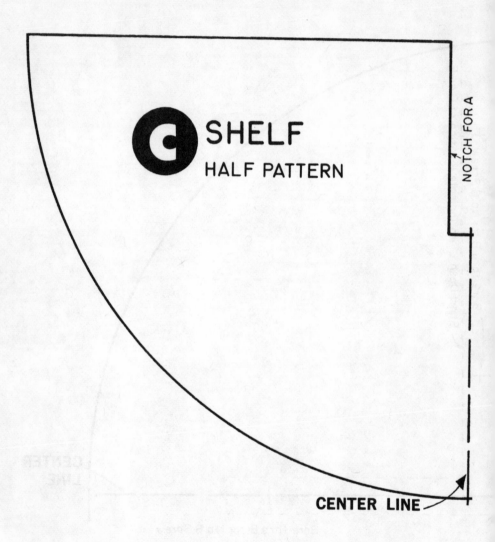

C SHELF
HALF PATTERN

NOTCH FOR A

CENTER LINE

HANDY - REFERENCE - LUMBER

PLYWOOD - FLAKEBOARD - HARDBOARD - MOULDINGS

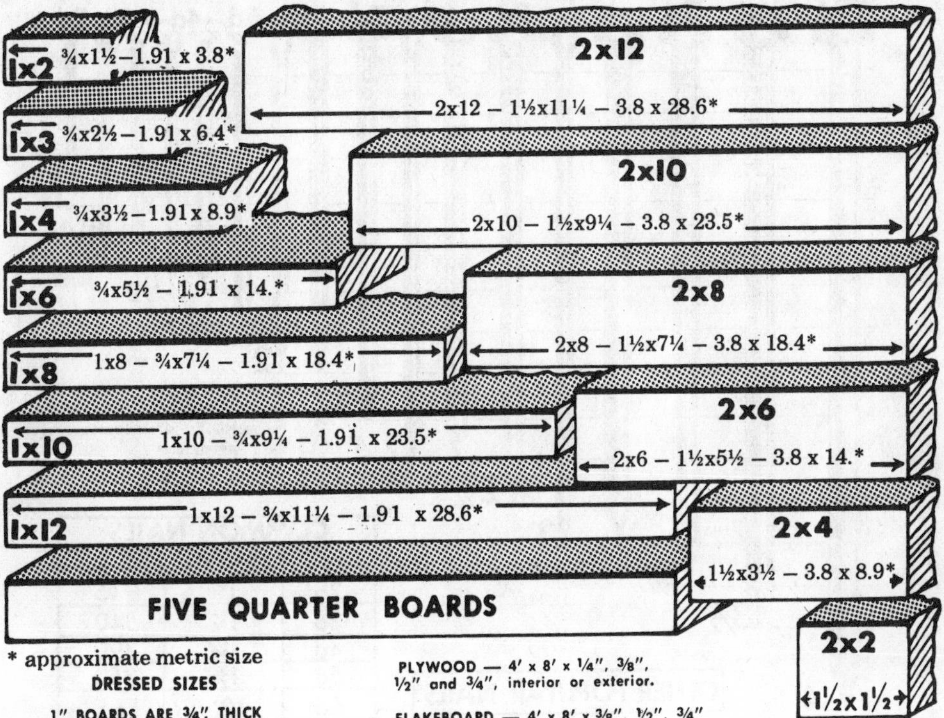

1x2 ¾x1½–1.91 x 3.8*
1x3 ¾x2½–1.91 x 6.4*
1x4 ¾x3½–1.91 x 8.9*
1x6 ¾x5½ – 1.91 x 14.*
1x8 1x8 – ¾x7¼ – 1.91 x 18.4*
1x10 1x10 – ¾x9¼ – 1.91 x 23.5*
1x12 1x12 – ¾x11¼ – 1.91 x 28.6*
FIVE QUARTER BOARDS
2x12
2x12 – 1½x11¼ – 3.8 x 28.6*
2x10
2x10 – 1½x9¼ – 3.8 x 23.5*
2x8
2x8 – 1½x7¼ – 3.8 x 18.4*
2x6
2x6 – 1½x5½ – 3.8 x 14.*
2x4
1½x3½ – 3.8 x 8.9*
2x2
1½x1½

* approximate metric size

DRESSED SIZES

1" BOARDS ARE ¾" THICK
2" BOARDS ARE 1½" THICK
5/4" BOARDS ARE 1-1/16" THICK.

PLYWOOD — 4' x 8' x ¼", ⅜", ½" and ¾", interior or exterior.

FLAKEBOARD — 4' x 8' x ⅜", ½", ¾"

HARDBOARD — 4' x 6', 4' x 8' x ⅛", ¼", standard and tempered.

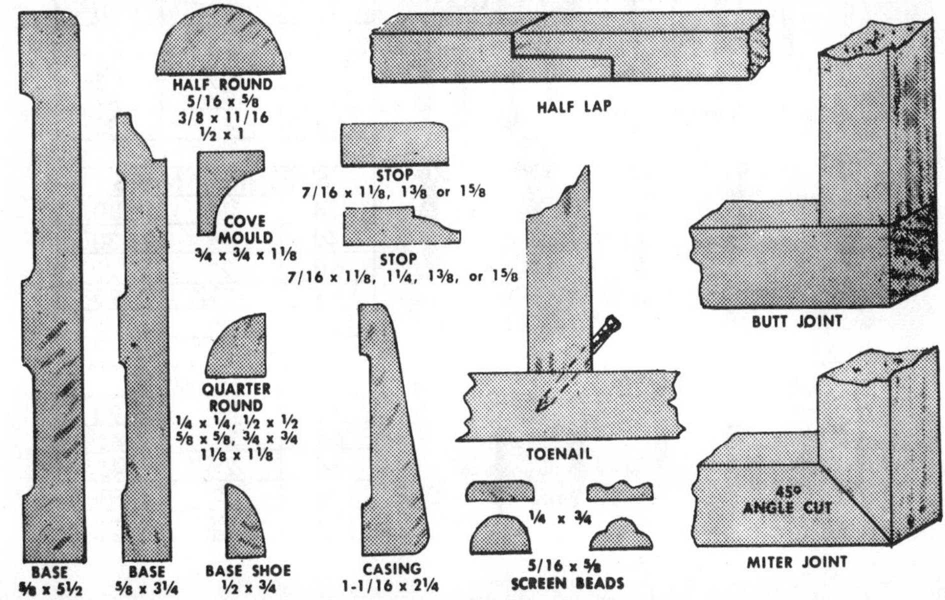

HALF ROUND
5/16 x ⅝
3/8 x 11/16
½ x 1
HALF LAP
STOP
7/16 x 1⅛, 1⅜ or 1⅝
COVE MOULD
¾ x ¾ x 1⅛
STOP
7/16 x 1⅛, 1¼, 1⅜, or 1⅝
BUTT JOINT
QUARTER ROUND
¼ x ¼, ½ x ½
⅝ x ⅝, ¾ x ¾
1⅛ x 1⅛
TOENAIL
¼ x ¾
45° ANGLE CUT
BASE
⅝ x 5½
BASE
⅝ x 3¼
BASE SHOE
½ x ¾
CASING
1-1/16 x 2¼
5/16 x ⅝
SCREEN BEADS
MITER JOINT

HANDY REFERENCE-NAILS

Common— Finishing—

20d 16d 12d 10d 9d 8d 7d 6d 5d 4d 3d 2d

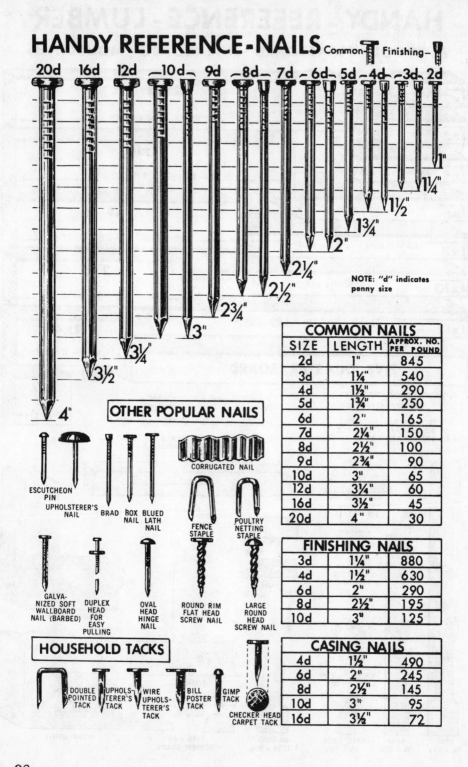

1"
1¼"
1½"
1¾"
2"
2¼"
2½"
2¾"
3"
3¼"
3½"
4"

NOTE: "d" indicates penny size

OTHER POPULAR NAILS

ESCUTCHEON PIN

UPHOLSTERER'S NAIL

BRAD

BOX NAIL

BLUED LATH NAIL

CORRUGATED NAIL

FENCE STAPLE

POULTRY NETTING STAPLE

GALVANIZED SOFT WALLBOARD NAIL (BARBED)

DUPLEX HEAD FOR EASY PULLING

OVAL HEAD HINGE NAIL

ROUND RIM FLAT HEAD SCREW NAIL

LARGE ROUND HEAD SCREW NAIL

HOUSEHOLD TACKS

DOUBLE POINTED TACK

UPHOLSTERER'S TACK

WIRE UPHOLSTERER'S TACK

BILL POSTER TACK

GIMP TACK

CHECKER HEAD CARPET TACK

COMMON NAILS

SIZE	LENGTH	APPROX. NO. PER POUND
2d	1"	845
3d	1¼"	540
4d	1½"	290
5d	1¾"	250
6d	2"	165
7d	2¼"	150
8d	2½"	100
9d	2¾"	90
10d	3"	65
12d	3¼"	60
16d	3½"	45
20d	4"	30

FINISHING NAILS

3d	1¼"	880
4d	1½"	630
6d	2"	290
8d	2½"	195
10d	3"	125

CASING NAILS

4d	1½"	490
6d	2"	245
8d	2½"	145
10d	3"	95
16d	3½"	72